T0171576

A Daughter's Desire,
A Mother's Worst Nightmare

GEETA MANGAL

iUniverse, Inc.
Bloomington

A Daughter's Desire, A Mother's Worst Nightmare

Copyright © 2012 Geeta Mangal

iUniverse books may be ordered through booksellers or by contacting:

iUniverse
1663 Liberty Drive
Bloomington, IN 47403
www.iuniverse.com
1-800-Authors (1-800-288-4677)

ISBN: 978-1-4502-9965-7 (sc)
ISBN: 978-1-4502-9967-1 (hc)
ISBN: 978-1-4502-9966-4 (e)

Printed in the United States of America

iUniverse rev. date: 01/20/2012

SHIVANI'S DEDICATION

This book is dedicated to my mother, Sharmela, whom I truly adore and admire, not only for giving me the gift of life, but for being the courageous and strongly independent woman she has become over the years.

I felt trapped in a maze. My mind, body, and soul were held captive by a man who claimed to love me. When the world turned its back on me, my mother was the only one who supported me every step of the way. My mother stood on the front line, putting her own welfare at risk, each day fighting like a soldier with her hands clasped in prayer, in hopes that my catastrophe would come to a halt and eternal bliss would enter my life.

My mother's prayers kept me alive to share my story. My mother's guidance and support have made me into the individual that I am today—a woman who possesses self-respect and exudes confidence. I can conquer the world now because of my guardian angel, my warrior, my idol.

"I love you, Mom."

— Shivani

Contents

Prologue

Shivani Ragunandan grew up in Guyana, in a small village called Rampur, Blairmont Estate which the locals called Rampoor Blairmont. Her parents were staunch believers in their Indo-Guyanese culture. Her childhood days were filled with lots of comfort, pleasure, and security, but most of all, love in abundance.

Shivani could recall growing up in the beautiful, two-story house built by her parents. The youngest of three children, she would wake up early in the morning to the sound of a rooster, followed by the smell of her mom's food. Shivani's mom, Sharmela, would be in the kitchen preparing food for her husband, Sunil, to take to work. He worked on a sugar plantation. He had to report to work by six o'clock in the morning every day. His primary source of transportation was a bicycle. He cycled to work 6 miles each day.

At the smell of her mom's homemade food, Shivani would jump out of bed and race to the kitchen, where her mom usually was by four in the morning. As her dad left for work, her mom would get Shivani and her siblings ready for school. These were the best days of Shivani's life.

After school, Shivani, her sister Seeta and brother Anil, and their cousins Angela, Ormela, Ryan, Lisa, and Arnold would make a stop at Nanny's (In Guyana, natives address the mother of their mom as Nanny and the father as Nana) house on their way home from school. Their favorite spot in Nanny's house was her kitchen. Nanny often made special afternoon snacks—"cassava pone" and fried green plantains, which are West Indian delights, and a special drink made out of lime, sugar, and crushed ice. Unfortunately, Sharmela did not grow up in the home of her biological mother, who passed when she was a child. She was also neglected by her father. She grew up with her maternal aunt who she referred to as her mother and Shivani refers to as Danpat, Nanny. Danpat, is addresses here after as Shivani's grandmother and Sharmela's mom.

Shivani's grandmother, Danpat, took pride in making these delicacies for her grandkids. Her grandfather, Nana Avinash, enjoyed watching with a stern eye. Nanny was a housewife caring for her family, while Nana worked in the sugar industry and as a farmer to provide financially for his family.

Shivani grew up having lots of friends in her neighborhood, school, and church. Every Sunday morning, "Mandir"—church—was essential for Sharmela. She would make "parsadaan," a sweet made from milk, sugar, and ghee, for Shivani and her siblings to take to Mandir as an offering to the gods. Sharmela would pick beautiful flowers from her garden and give them to the children to put on the statues of the god and goddess as a symbol of love.

Sharmela was a very strong, opinionated woman and very stern with her decisions. Upholding her family ties and caring for her family were her main focus.

At this time, Shivani was in her cocoon stage, as in the life cycle of a butterfly. She was the most radiant flower in Sharmela's rose garden. At the tender age of seven, her curiosity was at its peak. She always wanted to know whether there was a surprise and demanded some answers.

Sharmela tried to instill in Shivani that only when she grew older would she understand how a person's life was like a butterfly living in a garden. In its cocoon stage, a caterpillar needs shelter to protect it until it goes through a transformation and becomes a butterfly with wings strong enough to fly.

Shivani, however, was on a mission—the answers her mom gave her were not enough to satisfy her curiosity. She was destined for answers and a deeper understanding of why things were structured the way they were in her community.

Chapter 1

INDO — GUYANESE CULTURE, VALUES, AND TRADITION

(Growing up in the Republic of Guyana)

Shivani was brought up in the old-school way, in which tradition and culture are defined. She grew up in a Hindu home, where all rules were set forth by her parents. The rules had to be followed. She did not ask any questions; she just abided by them. She knew that if she asked questions, then her parents or other family members would interpret her curiosity in a whole different way. They would think she was being rebellious or rude to their culture and tradition.

Shivani always thought the rules held a double standard, since more restrictions was placed on girls than boys. Her father always told her, "A man can climb through many windows. But the first window that a girl goes through, her reputation will be tarnished for life." In other words, a man could have as many women as he pleased and make many mistakes, but a woman absolutely could not. When a woman made a mistake, everyone spread rumors about her and tarnished her reputation by exaggerating the truth. Women in traditional Hindu culture are like soldiers, vigilantly guarding their daughters from making any mistakes.

As a child, Shivani was not allowed to be outside past dusk unless she had parental supervision. She could not wear shorts, tightly fitted jeans, or any skirts above her knees, because the female body had to be covered appropriately. Sharmela made certain that Shivani did not develop any relationships with the opposite sex and that she remained focused on school. She was also taught that she needed to address her elders as "Auntie" and "Uncle," even if they were not blood relatives. Showing affection outdoors was also not acceptable; it was considered disrespectful to elders and family members.

In Shivani's mind, these were the necessities of life and the survival kit to get through life's challenges—having respect for elders, addressing and treating everyone in the community as family, and following culture and tradition. This is the foundation of the Hindu way of living life.

Shivani never questioned the decisions of her elders. She needed to trust their judgment because they were older and wiser. In Shivani's Indo-Guyanese culture, women were an asset and were always worshiped by their husbands and children. The woman was the family's "Maha

Latchmi," the goddess of wealth and prosperity. As Shivani's father would say, "Your mother is the light of our home."

Her father also told her, "A woman's character is her beauty. Maintain your dignity and never let shame come upon us." Her parents warned her not to disgrace them, because they would disown her if she did. They would have been embarrassed if their daughter did not live up to the standards that were set forth by the community. In Shivani's opinion, her family was more concerned about how people in their society and culture viewed them; rather than about how the family saw themselves.

As in the life cycle of butterflies, Shivani was still in her cocoon stage. Her parents sheltered her because they felt that she wasn't ready to spread her wings. Her parents felt that it would do more harm than good to allow her to come out early. When her culture and traditions were firmly embedded in her, she would be ready to take on the world.

*   *   *

Shivani's family lived in a small village called Rampoor Blairmont, located on the west coast of Berbice, Guyana, in South America. Rampoor Blairmont was surrounded by a sugar plantation. Shivani's father, Sunil, worked in the sugar industry.

Bicycles were the main form of private transportation, while locomotives carried people and goods for longer distances for the underdeveloped village, where the people worked diligently to provide for their families. Primary occupations included farming, fishing, raising poultry, and operating local businesses. The cobblestone roads made it very difficult for cars and other forms of transportation to travel into the village. Therefore, bicycling was the main form of private transportation. The local residents also used donkey carts or would walk to their destination to sell their products. They would call out to the other residents as they passed by.

There were not many stores in this small community. In order to get to the marketplace, residents needed to cross the Berbice River in a motor launch, which is a small boat made out of wood. The interior of the motor launch has benches for people to sit on. It was about a twenty-minute ride to the marketplace, which was in the next city over, called New Amsterdam.

Most people preferred to buy from local business owners. The advantage of buying locally was that residents could pay by "trust." Buyers could take products and pay the seller at a later date. The seller would make a note that the customer still owed money. Business owners considered this a binding agreement. Another advantage to buying locally was that the residents could expect fresh fruits, vegetables, and fish to be delivered to their doorsteps without ever leaving home.

The community was small. Everyone knew each other and looked out for each other. They shared whatever they had with love. One incident resonated in Shivani's heart from the time she was six years old. Shivani's mother, Sharmela, used to put Shivani and her siblings to bed early. Her father, Sunil, would leave them to volunteer with a committee called "Vigilante." This was a small organization that provided watchmen for the village. The volunteers secured the town from six in the evening to six in the morning. The men would walk through each settlement with hand lamps, looking out for suspicious activities involving theft or other crimes. The citizens would use codes such as three drum rolls, which warned residents to be alert because intruders were around. Shivani's community had created a home for which Shivani felt loved, safe and protected from harm. This is one of the most memorable experiences she had because she has not experienced one such as this after her move.

When Shivani resided there in the early 1980s, the demographics of Rampoor Blairmont were 90 percent Indo-Guyanese and 10 percent Afro- Guyanese. The most-practiced religion was Hinduism, followed by Islam and then Christianity. The community was filled with love.

When Shivani was eight, her family migrated to the Cayman Islands in search of a better life for their children-bearing in mind Shivani family was living in a poverty- stricken village where they were

4

little opportunity available to the citizens. It did not take Shivani long to notice that both men and women were employed in the Cayman Islands, whereas in Guyana, women were limited to being housewives. She also noticed some changes in their family life. Her father began contributing equally to household chores instead of relying on Sharmela. When Shivani questioned this shift in family values, her mother stated, "Changes come with time, and this is a different era."

They lived in the Cayman Islands for nearly six years before moving to the United States. Shivani was thirteen when her family moved to New Jersey. Her parents decided to move so Shivani and her siblings could have a better life, including the opportunity to go to college. In the Cayman Islands at that time, there were no colleges or universities. Shivani's parents valued education and steadily supported the children throughout their educational voyage. Shivani and her siblings were fortunate to have the opportunity to further their education.

Once in New Jersey, Shivani's imagination ran wild. What could this new oasis have to offer the already enchanted life she led? The community was larger, and Shivani immediately recognized that its members were more independent, free, and diverse. The governing laws were equally balanced for both genders. Her mom, Sharmela, now worked two jobs and did not spend as much time at home as she had in the past.

Little did Shivani knew that her mom was determined that she follow and maintain the traditions they had followed in Guyana. Shivani's family kept a low profile. Shivani was not allowed to attend sleepovers or parties. She concentrated on her education, working diligently to make her dreams come true and make her parents proud of her.

Starting high school in America, Shivani was exposed to friends who smoked, drank, used drugs, and made out with their boyfriends in the streets. This was a new American reality, since in Guyana, these behaviors were completely inappropriate. If a girl was caught engaging in these behaviors, there were consequences, such as being disowned. Shivani knew she could not pursue this way of life because her family wanted her to preserve her culture. Adopting the American culture was not an option. Almost everything that Shivani had learned was unacceptable in relationships and marriages was acceptable in America.

American culture was enticing in other ways. Shivani was not given the independence to try out new things, like clothing, foods, and nightlife. Her parents never allowed it. She was careful not to follow in her friends' footsteps. She just stayed focused on going to college.

By the time Shivani entered college in 2001, her mom and dad were working two jobs while making sure all the children remained disciplined, took part in fasting, and went to Mandir. Dating, especially, was strictly forbidden. Sharmela had other plans for Shivani's love life.

In the Indo-Guyanese culture, arranged marriages were the norm. Shivani's grandmother, Nanny Danpat, had been married to Nana Avinash when she was thirteen years old. At this tender age, she was successful in raising a family, managing a home, and taking care of her husband and children.

Even as a grandmother, Danpat was very beautiful, with her long, black, wavy hair and a golden-brown complexion. She was pretty set in her ways and had a knack for straightening her children out with her sharp-toned voice. She had the remedy for everything. She always told Shivani, "You don't need to go to the doctor; it's a waste of money!" Nanny delivered all of her grandbabies in her own home and used cures made of local grass and herbal supplements when her children would catch fever. Shivani could only imagine that raising a family had been tough when Danpat was young, so her Nanny had to use limited resources and cut down on cost whenever possible.

Shivani's grandfather, Avinash, did his part in raising all of his children and grandchildren as well. He had a strong presence with his physique alone, towering over other people at six feet, four inches tall. He had a taupe complexion and a very thick Indian accent.

Avinash always carried a long "whip" from the stem of a tree called a "Black Sage". The slender stick was about five feet in length. He used this whip for disciplining his grandchildren—but only if his rules were not followed. Nanny protected the children from the whip in the same way parents protect their children from dangerous household items such medicines and cleaning supplies. The whip would go everywhere with him, especially when he went farming across the river , using it as a weapon to fight off his enemies. It would make an indescribable sound as Avinash swung it over their bodies. One hit would give anyone a sting for an hour or two. Everyone was afraid of the whip.

The whip was a disciplinary mechanism that was used throughout the school system in the Republic of Guyana. Parents reinforced this discipline as a consequence if a child misbehaved. The whip seemed to be successful because it created fear in children.

Another disciplinary mechanism that families used to create obedient children was the act of disowning. By disowning a child, the family attempted to create boundaries and force children to take responsibility their actions. Asking her grandmother questions about their culture, Shivani discovered that Nanny had disowned a daughter.

Although she stood only four feet, eleven inches tall, Nanny's daughter Lilawatie was a risk taker, the black sheep of the bunch. Lilawatie was Nanny's third daughter. She was seventeen years old when she was betrothed, and was unhappy in her arranged marriage. Lilawatie hated the fact that her husband was always controlling her. She liked to go out, but her husband wanted her to stay at home and perform the duties of a housewife. Her very traditional husband, Ramesh would complain about her behavior and talk about his expectations with Nanny, in hopes that she could talk to Lilawatie and influence a change.

Nanny spoke to Lilawatie about her behavior, but this did not change Lilawatie's disobedient ways. So her parents told her that she was no longer allowed to come back home.

Months later, Nanny found out that Lilawatie abandoned her husband and remarried to someone from another race and had two children.

Shivani's grandparents had excluded their daughter Lilawatie from their home and lives permanently. Lilawatie's battle to belong to her family became a failed effort. Shivani's mother recalled that the family became distorted after Lilawatie's exit. Sharmela and her siblings strongly desired to continue communication, but they could not. Lilawatie kept trying to mend the broken ties, but she could not. The family had closed that chapter. After the family migrated to the United States, contact with Lilawatie was lost.

Arranged marriages have existed in Hindu and other cultures around the world for quite some time. An individual seeks a lifelong partner, and because of restrictions on socializing between the genders, the only means to become acquainted is to rely on family and friends to introduce one person to another. In such a situation, a person can only hope that the family will find someone who will best suit the person's innermost desires, goals, and values. The outcome of an arranged match depends on how compatible the partners are and how much they are willing to sacrifice to ensure that their union is one of prosperity.

Hopes for a compatible match are not always realized. Young girls between the ages of thirteen and eighteen can be taken out of school and forced into marriage with men they barely know. To this day, many people within the Indo-Guyanese culture practice arranged marriages.

Shivani's Nanny instilled many cultural values and principles in her children at a very young age. She made it very clear if they did not take heed of their upbringing, they would be considered outcasts and would be disowned.

Nanny had three boys and seven girls. She paid extra attention to her seven girls because, in Indo-Guyanese culture, a woman's innocence and purity is respected by the family and is strongly encouraged. The reason given for this is to preserve cultural identity and adherence to family obligations. Shivani's mother and aunts all went through the process of arranged marriage and had their own outcomes. Two of Shivani's aunts were widowed, one died, and three, including Shivani's mother, are still happily married today.

Shivani's widowed aunts continued their cultural traditions. They did not remarry when their husbands died. They invested time and effort into holding their families together and striving for betterment in a new land that gave them the opportunity for educational advancement, freedom of speech, and other rights.

In recent years, Shivani has become more aware of the challenges her aunts encountered. Their husbands did not have a goal set in place for what they wanted do with their lives. Shivani's uncles gambled, drank frequently, and abused their wives.

Nanny did not divulge these problems to outsiders. She believed that it was her responsibility to mend matters between the couples, and not the responsibility of an outsider who wouldn't have any insight on the parties.

Sharmela remembers Danpat sending her off to another village to help her sisters with child care and domestic duties for a couple of weeks at a time. In her village, getting an education was considered secondary. For her family, building a community with love superseded everything.

Danpat was generous and had a charismatic character. She was a phenomenal woman, and her legacy lived on in the lives of the fruits she bore. Now Sharmela is responsible for keeping the family tradition. She embodies all her mother's spirit and wisdom.

Shivani's aunt Heema, the fourth-oldest child, also followed in her mother's footsteps and continued good deeds. After one sister's tragic death, she adopted those nieces and nephews.

Aunt Bobita, the third-oldest daughter of Danpat, she became the family hero as Danpat would say because she freed her siblings from the poverty-stricken village in Guyana, and they all ventured to the Cayman Islands in search for a better life.

Aunt Rekhaa, the seventh-oldest child of Danpat, stood in the face of adversity and raised her sons without any assistance from her husband. He used to drink excessively and mistreat her.

Aunt Bindie, the oldest child of Danpat, was led astray by friends and her husband. She never had an opportunity to unite with her other siblings, and did not live up to the standards and expectations her mother had set forth for all of her children.

Aunt Bhogwatte, the sixth-oldest daughter, was the family's spiritual leader who served as a peacemaker.

Shivani at the age of twenty-two had accomplished most of the goals her parents expected. She was ready to embark on yet another educational journey: achieving a master's degree. As she fought really hard to make her dream a reality, her parents supported her every step of the way and prayed for her success in all endeavors. Her parents envisioned a bright and prosperous future for their daughter as they watched her aiming for higher goals.

At the same time, Shivani had reached the age for marriage, and her mother Sharmela was ready to advise her about finding a husband that fit *all* of Sharmela's criteria. Shivani had been dreading this day because she knew it was coming soon. But she never could understand why her family needed to find her a husband.

Traditionally in Indo-Guyanese society, when girls reach their teenage years, parents begin to play matchmaker in order to ensure their daughters' security. To succeed in matchmaking, families must preserve their daughters' innocence and purity. So Sharmela kept her eyes and ears open to make sure Shivani did not go out with friends or date boys. She also began giving small lectures about family values, upbringing, and the Indian caste system. Sharmela forbade Shivani to date a boy of another race, for it would bring shame upon her family. Sharmela refused to allow her daughter to lose value.

Discussion of arranged marriage would always lead to an argument between Shivani and Sharmela, since they did not see things the same way. For Sharmela, having a good life meant that a partner shared the same values and culture. It had nothing to do with wealth or earning a higher education. Sharmela encouraged Shivani to pursue a higher education because she valued education, but at the same time it wasn't a defining factor used when searching for Shivani's husband. Sharmela was confident that Shivani would be fully capable of providing for a family because she was highly educated.

Sharmela did not believe in true love or love at first sight. It was more important to follow culture and tradition rather than, as she called it, having a "fantasy life." She believed that once a person was paired with someone, that person would learn about his or her partner and, eventually, love would come, since love was secondary. Having a partner from the same culture was what was essential for a marriage to last a lifetime.

A lasting marriage based on shared values is the ultimate goal for parents when pairing a young man with a young woman. Parents rely on the church and Hindu bylaws. The prospective husband or wife must attend Mandir and follow Hindu beliefs, which hold worshiping God and parents in the highest regard. Mandir plays an important role in Hindus culture since it is the foundation for a good life. Indo-Guyanese believe that seeking spiritual guidance is always the best avenue to use when difficulties are encountered.

Shivani wanted the liberty to make her own choices, and especially to choose her ideal life partner. The "fantasy life" seemed like a much better option than an arranged life.

Customarily, Sharmela had the right to choose the person Shivani was to marry. Sharmela did not want Shivani to go to college and fall in love with someone the family did not approve of. It was always her mother's desire to find Shivani a man who was the mirror image of her dad—a perfect man who was religious, respectful, traditional, and followed every bit of Indo-Guyanese culture.

The topic of arranged marriage was an uncomfortable and awkward subject for Shivani to discuss with her parents because she knew that what she had to say would be of no value to them. If she gave any input, then she would come across as disrespectful of her parents' wishes. She wanted to avoid arguments with her mom, so she did not want to speak her mind too often.

Deep down, she knew that an arranged marriage was not her desire. However, her heart did strive to find a man such as her father. She just wanted someone who would respect, love, and cherish her; someone she could trust her secrets to, who would be the rock she could count on in tough situations.

Strangely, even with all the tradition Shivani had adopted, she still attracted a person who was the complete opposite of her father. Her father always said, "Go with your first instincts." Shivani's instincts warned her about this person's arrogance and pretense. He was phony and would go all out to make himself look good in the face of adversity. How Shivani wished, later, that she had listened to that inner voice, the one that softly spoke of the deceit and arrogance that was before her.

As Shivani expected, one day her mother called her into the living room to tell her the plans they had made for her love life. Shivani refused to adhere to the arranged marriage proposal, which made her mother angry.

Sharmela: Shivani, your father and I think it's time for us to find you a husband.

Shivani: Mom, why can't I find my own husband?

Sharmela: Shivani, you know why. That is not part of our culture. We don't want you to find your own husband because he may not meet our cultural standards and our family's expectations. We as parents will be able to decide who will be a perfect match for you.

Shivani: Mom, are you saying you don't trust my judgment? I want to be able to take part in this decision. As you know, this is a life-changing decision.

Sharmela (getting angry): Shivani, our conversation has ended. You are disrespecting us as parents.

Shivani, now highly upset, turned and walked away, filled with disappointment.

Chapter 2

Love:
The Wedding Proposal

It was a beautiful summer afternoon in August 2007. The wind blew gently through the fruit trees that Shivani's dad, Sunil, had planted in their backyard. She watched the birds peck the pears and apples off the trees. As she rocked back and forth on the swing, she stared up in the sky and saw a beautiful rainbow. This signified the promise of a happy ending for her, especially since she had been through a long journey.

Later that afternoon, she relaxed on her bed and looked through the blue, velvet-covered family photo album her mother had made for her. Most of the pictures were of Shivani and her two siblings at family gatherings. Shivani was the youngest of the three.

She gently turned the pages, being careful not to damage the photos inside. She found an old picture that was not mounted in the album, but somehow stuck in the middle of a page. The picture was ripped on the edges, with blotches of coffee stains in the center and also on the faces of the individuals. Despite the stains, she could still make out the two faces in the picture. One was herself, and the other was someone Shivani had cared for deeply. She immediately turned the photo face-down.

Shivani started having flashbacks after she saw that picture. Tears streamed down her face. Her heart skipped a beat and an orchestra of horror movie theme music played in her head. Her body became alert and scared stiff. Shivani remembered the exact place and time of the picture. She vividly recalled how she had felt at the moment it was taken. It was as though she was reliving her past all over again.

Shivani's mood instantly changed. She had always thought that the isolated behavior of an individual could not change the dynamics of someone else's mind and perspective on life, but life had proven that her theory was wrong.

Shivani had also thought that she had gotten over this hurdle in her life. Now, she quickly shut the album and ran as fast as she could to a place where she felt safe—her mother's bedroom. She shut the door tightly. The flashbacks wouldn't stop running through her head. She could only hear the echo of an intruder's voice calling out her name as his footsteps got closer to her. Her body trembled with fear, and she tightly shut her eyes, hoping she would awaken from this nightmare.

There was a knock on the door. She was silent. "Shivani," her mom said, "dinner is ready."

Shivani quickly wiped the tears from her cheeks and answered, "I will be right down."

She ate dinner quickly that night and then, oddly enough, ran to her room to continue looking through the album.

Shivani gently opened the cover but did not turn over the picture. As she browsed, she came across a photo of her eighth birthday. She remembered that day like it was yesterday. Those early years were her magical years, the years she yearned to relive but never could. Those were the years when her innocence was at its peak, when the world was perfect. There had been no pain, hurt, or sadness in her life. People had lived like family in Guyana and had helped each other to build their community.

As this evening came to a close, Shivani's phone rang. It was her friend Monique waiting for her to come outside. Monique was one of the few friends that Shivani's parents were comfortable with and trust with the welfare of their daughter. Shivani closed the album, tucked it under her bed covers, and left. The past was too fresh in her mind because of the photos.

Luckily, as the night progressed, her memories faded away and her attention became focused on the fun she and Monique were having.

Monique was a close friend and someone Shivani confided in about certain situations. Monique had come into Shivani's life just in the nick of time. She was one of the few friends Shivani could reach out to whenever Shivani needed to find resolution to conflicts. Monique's personality and positive energy fascinated Shivani, and Shivani gravitated toward her. Shivani had always tended to gravitate toward those who touched her life and saw the best in her, even when she could not.

*   *   *

Shivani's mom made sure that Shivani attended many cultural gatherings that occurred at the mandir and at peoples' private residences.

Such meetings provided opportunities for Sharmela to meet Shivani's prospective husband. It was Sharmela's belief that attending Mandir regularly would lead to finding a good husband within the church.

Sharmela also invested time in teaching Shivani how to cook authentic cultural dishes and delicacies. Shivani's mom would always say to her, "You are ready for marriage when you know how to cook." Sharmela showed her how to skillfully fasten and wear Indian clothing. She also taught Shivani how to sing songs at the Mandir and instructed her in the "Bhagavad Gita", which is one of the oldest and most sacred books for Hindus. It was her mother's intention to instill in Shivani a strong cultural identity and teach her never to lose sight of her values.

In this way, Shivani's mother performed all of the necessary duties any Indo-Guyanese mother would do in preparing her daughter for marriage. Sharmela never anticipated that this marriage would turn into a gruesome experience.

Kevin and Shivani were introduced in September by her cousin Dan, the eldest son of Shivani's paternal aunt. Her cousin had spent the Labor Day weekend at Shivani's home in New Jersey. Sharmela had suggested that it would be much simpler for them to drive him to his family home in Brooklyn, New York instead of him taking the bus and train.

En route to Brooklyn, Dan told Shivani about a friend who was looking to settle down. He mentioned this to Shivani at first hand because he was unsure of where Shivani and her family had stand on arrange marriage. Shivani quickly confirmed her family's beliefs to Dan. He recommended that she meet this friend. He knew how strict her dad was when it came to her, so he was cautious not to say anything to Shivani's family at that time without her consent. He only wanted to cover his tracks.

Dan eventually called Kevin from the car and told him that he was getting a ride home. Dan also told Kevin that Shivani was in the car and that he would be stopping by to pick up a CD. So Dan asked Shivani's brother Anil, who was driving, if Anil could stop by Kevin's apartment on their way to pick up the CD, since Kevin lived only a couple of blocks away from Dan. Anil had no idea that Dan sole purpose was for Shivani and Kevin to get a glimpse of each other, so he agreed to stop by.

When they arrived at Kevin's apartment, Kevin came to the car and introduced himself to Shivani, Anil, and their father Sunil, who was also in the car. The introduction happened quickly; Sunil and Anil just nodded their heads. Kevin handed Dan the CD and flashed his captivating eyes at Shivani as they drove off. In this way, Kevin exhibited traditional Indo-Guyanese cultural values, respecting the fact that he was not allowed to engage in any form of conversation with a woman without her parents' permission.

All Shivani could think about that night was Kevin and the possibility of learning more about him. Dan had said many wonderful things about him. Shivani thought that the feelings must have been mutual, because her cousin called that night to tell her that Kevin thought she was attractive and wanted to learn more about her.

Shivani told Dan that he had to let her parents know, because of the conversational taboo. Shortly after, Dan contacted Sharmela and told her about Kevin's interest in Shivani and attended Mandir regularly. "Mandir"—that was critical to Sharmela in finding Shivani a mate. So arrangements were made for Kevin to visit Shivani's parents. Three weeks later, the time had come for the introduction.

Compared to Shivani's petite five-foot frame, Kevin stood tall at five feet, eleven inches. His dark brown complexion perfectly complemented his wavy black hair. Shivani could remember his beautiful brown eyes piercing into her soul. She had been fairly impressed with him at first sight. Kevin seemed sweet and innocent, with great sense of humor.

Instantly, Kevin won Shivani's parents over with his use of cultural protocol. Sharmela and Sunil were addressed with "Sita Ram" and a head bow, which is the sign of utmost respect. ("Sita Ram" is a simple phrase that Indians use according to Sanatana Vedic Dharma, Hindu's personal obligations, to greet their Hindu brothers and sisters.) Kevin also practiced customary American gestures, such as shaking hands and hugging or kissing on the cheek.

During the meeting, Shivani's parents discussed with Kevin their family's upbringing, cultural values, and background. About four or five hours after their initial meeting, a subsequent meeting was arranged for the following week so all the parties could meet and discuss engagement plans. Since Kevin did not have parents in the United States at the time, his legal guardian would accompany him.

It was a beautiful Saturday afternoon in mid-October. The sun brightly lit the sky, the birds chirped a wonderful song, and the breeze gently blew the red and orange leaves through the streets. Shivani opened her bedroom window and sat waiting for Kevin's arrival. She wore a lavender, button-down shirt and a pair of khaki-colored capri pants, plus two gold bangles Sharmela had given her on her sixteenth birthday.

Shivani felt accomplished, having arrived at this milestone in her life. She had completed college, obtained a full-time job, and was working toward a master's degree. She also felt that she had obeyed her parents' wishes by allowing them to select her lifelong partner.

Shivani had followed all the principles of her Dharm, the Hindu term for a person's obligations, calling, and duties. Since this was going to be her first time meeting Kevin's family, she had to show that the Indo-Guyanese culture was embedded in her. She had been careful when selecting clothing to wear on this day. She knew that she shouldn't wear an outfit that was too revealing, because traditionally, the body must be fully clothed.

When Kevin and his family arrived, Sharmela greeted them at the door and led them into the living room. Shivani had been told that she had to stay in her room while the family discussed his marriage proposal to Shivani. It annoyed her that she could not voice her opinion, more so because she couldn't hear any of the discussion. She even pressed her ear to the wall to try and listen in on their conversation, but had no luck. This discussion included only her parents, Kevin, and his guardian.

This is typical of the customs relating to Indo-Guyanese arranged marriages. Sharmela shared with her daughter an experience she had at the age of sixteen, when her parents arranged her marriage to Sunil. He was twenty-four years old at the time. Sharmela remembered that she took no part in what transpired between the families. All she could recall was her mother, Danpat, calling her upstairs, in Guyana, the family rooms are located upstairs opposed to the U.S, where they are located downstairs, and requesting her thoughts about her new husband. Sharmela just stood there as everyone stared at her, patiently waiting for her reply. There were more than ten people packed in their family room, because Sunil had brought his parents, siblings, and a couple close friends to the meeting.

Sharmela was not impressed with Sunil at first sight. He did not look like the person she had expected to fall in love with. He was short and dark-skinned. However, she was too afraid to say anything since her objections might have come across as offensive.

Love eventually came into their relationship. Today, Shivani's parents have been married for over thirty-four years. Sunil is the only man Sharmela ever had a relationship with. Marriage definitely was not an easy road for Sharmela to travel with Sunil, either, since there have been many obstacles, such as family issues with her in-laws and adjusting to Sunil's ways and habits.

When Kevin first met Shivani's family, he was polite, generous, and spoke with soothing words. His manner was very much like Sunil's. Kevin addressed Sharmela and Sunil "Mom" and "Dad," and appeared very religious because he was knowledgeable about Hindu scriptures. Kevin, Sharmela, and Sunil had a long conversation. Shivani's parents described their expectations of a son-in-law to Kevin. Only when Kevin expressed his interest in joining their family was Shivani finally called into the room.

Kevin told Shivani that he appreciated her family and felt that God had answered his prayers by bringing him into their home. He also said he had already made his decision and wanted Shivani for his wife.

This was a new beginning for Shivani. At that time, she felt that perhaps her prayers had been answered and that Kevin could be the person she would spend the rest of her life with. She had full faith in God, her parents, and her culture and tradition.

After the families met, the engagement date still had not been decided upon, since Kevin's family had to consult their priest and satisfy other obligations. Meantime, Shivani's parents wanted to ensure that the couple did not have any close contact before the formal engagement and marriage. This wasn't what Shivani wanted. Even though an arranged marriage was not what Shivani had hoped for her life, she had accepted Kevin's proposal. Now everything was moving too fast. She had just met Kevin one month previously and hardly knew him, yet they were close to becoming engaged!

In the following month, Sunil granted Kevin permission to visit Shivani and for them to communicate over the phone. Kevin and Shivani were not allowed to meet anywhere other than at her home, under parental supervision.

One day, Shivani's mother summoned her to the living room and told her that they needed to talk. Sharmela said that the date for Shivani's engagement had been set. Shivani was furious. "Mom, this is not fair! Can I at least get to know him?"

Sharmela said, "No! How much time do you need to get to know him? At least you know what he looks like. Isn't that enough? Your father and I never met before we were married. People take a lifetime to know each other."

Shivani couldn't believe what she was hearing. She wanted her mother to understand her position. Shivani said, "That was a very long time ago. Mom, what if I don't like him?"

Her mom was very stern in her position. "Shivani, I have spoken. You young people these days always think about 'love.' What about happiness and having a good life?"

Sharmela went on to say that she didn't like Kevin visiting Shivani without an engagement being settled. Sharmela believed that there should be a promise of marriage and a wedding date in place before a relationship was allowed to progress. It was a disgrace to the family for the relationship to continue unless these arrangements were made.

Shivani was extremely unhappy about the entire situation. Mostly what made her uncomfortable was not having a voice. Her family became increasingly upset with her because they felt she was rebelling against their authority and their tradition. Nonetheless, Shivani followed through on her parent's wishes. Her heart's desire was to please her parents.

After the conversation with her mother, Shivani spoke to Kevin about Sharmela's wishes. Kevin said that he wanted to continue seeing her and would do whatever it took, even if the ceremony had to be performed in a week or two.

Shivani's parents and Kevin's family met again during the Thanksgiving holiday. Shivani assumed all obligations were satisfied, because Kevin and Shivani were engaged on December 4, 2004, approximately two and a half months after they first met. The engagement ceremony was performed in the traditional Indo-Guyanese style. This includes a promise of loyalty that the bride and groom make to each other in front of God and the priest. After this vow is made, a couple is granted permission to see each other more often. The partners complete the other half of their rites in a traditional marriage ceremony.

During the ceremony, Shivani and Kevin exchanged rings and prayed together for prosperity in their relationship.

Chapter 3

Marriage: Traditional Indo-Guyanese Weddings

Hindu weddings can take up to four days, since different rituals must be performed before the grand celebration whereby the couple formalizes their union. Once a wedding date is set, the parents of the bride and groom consult with a Hindu priest. The priest has to refer to his sacred books to verify if the ceremony can be held on the date and time that the parties have selected. It is believed that the ceremony has to be performed when the moon and planets are favorable. This is determined according to the Hindu Vedic calendar, which outlines days when a marriage ceremony should be performed. These dates are called "lagan" dates. A similar practice is also performed for the engagement to clear all obstacles and check for compatibility. Hindus believe it is very important to adhere to this tradition or obstacles could occur in the marriage.

The marriage rituals are divided into three parts—pre-wedding customs, the wedding-day ceremony, and post-wedding rituals. All three phases have significance. The pre-wedding celebration mainly includes the engagement. The wedding day ceremony involves several traditional rituals, each having its own symbolism and with everyone playing a role.

The most important aspect of a Hindu wedding is the seven vows recited by the bride and groom as they walk around the sacred fire. The fire is important because it symbolizes worship of and communication with "Dewa Agni " the god of fire. While the seven vows are read by the priest, the bride and groom take the vows before God. These seven promises are expected to be the foundation of the marriage. The vows represent the loyalty, love, and commitment the couple will eventually share in their married life.

Followers of Hinduism believe that if a married couple recites the seven vows around the "havan kund," a fire flaring out of a pyramid-like construction made out of copper, they will remain together for a lifetime. Generally, before taking the seven vows, the bride is seated on the right-hand side of the groom. After reciting her vows, the bride shifts to the left-hand side, symbolizing that she is now closer to his heart.

The groom makes the first four offerings, while the bride delivers the three subsequent offerings to the fire. The seven vows the couple makes are as follows:

<u>Step 1</u>

Vow to provide a prosperous living for the household and avoid those who might hinder their healthy living.

<u>Step 2</u>

Vow to develop their physical, mental, and spiritual powers in order to lead a lifestyle that is healthy.

<u>Step 3</u>

Vow to earn a living and increase their earning power through righteous and proper means.

<u>Step 4</u>

Vow to acquire knowledge, happiness, and harmony through mutual love, respect, understanding, and faith. The bride and groom are promising to respect each other's decisions when there is a disagreement and learn how to work through problems.

<u>Step 5</u>

Vow to expand their heredity by having children, for whom they will be responsible. They also pray to be blessed with healthy, honest, and brave children.

<u>Step 6</u>

Vow to pray for the longevity of their marriage and also for self-control of the mind, body, and soul.

<u>Step 7</u>

Vow to be true and loyal to each other and remain companions and best of friends for a lifetime.

The post-wedding ceremony includes the reception, which is the most emotional moment of the wedding. The bride leaves her parents and other family members to take her first step toward her new life in her husband's home. When the bride reaches her new home, she is welcomed with games and everyone makes merry. Since Kevin's parents were not in the United States, Shivani's parents still followed tradition by arranging for his family to use the home of Seeta, Shivani's sister, as the location for the reception festivities.

It had always been Shivani's desire to have a grand celebration and experience the bliss and serenity that come with marriage. Her parents had granted her this grand celebration because they were happy for her. "You graduated from college," her mother said. "We are proud of you." Then Sharmela burst into tears.

In August, Shivani's parents and brother Anil hosted her traditional Indo-Guyanese wedding. The ceremony took place in her parents' backyard. It was a beautiful morning, but the night before, Shivani had a sleepless night. Her body was covered with yellow, scented powder called saffron, delicately applied by five beautiful young girls under the age of twelve— her niece Reshma and cousins Abigail, Elizabeth, Sarah, and Jennifer. The powder symbolized purity of the mind, soul, and body.

Nadira was assigned to be Shivani's caretaker the night before the wedding. Nadira had known Shivani as a little girl growing up in Guyana, when Nadira taught at the Rampeur Blairmont Primary School. The two women slept on the floor and reminisced about the past. They had a lot of catching up to do, since they hadn't seen each other in a long time.

This was one of the many sacred rituals performed before the wedding ceremony. In Indo-Guyanese culture, close family members and friends play a major role during the wedding and even after the couple is married. The delegated individuals are people from whom the bride and groom will seek advice in the future when problems arise within the marriage.

On her wedding day, Shivani was decked out in a beautifully radiant yellow sari. The sari was delicately wrapped around her body by her dear aunt, Mala, who pleated every fold with accuracy and precision. She also applied Shivani's makeup and adorned her body with all the necessary accessories. Smiling, she said to Shivani, "You only get married once in a lifetime. Some people are not fortunate to have a traditional and extravagant celebration such as yours. The ceremonies have to be performed according to strict Hindu ordinance. This is your day to smile and feel beautiful. You are going to be a married woman as of today. You need to be strong, because it is not a straight road to ride in marriage. There will be dead ends, turns, and even turbulence."

Shivani understood that it was not going to be perfect, but she was confident that with the qualities she and Kevin both possessed, it would be manageable.

Before the ceremony, there were many friends and well-wishers who wanted to come inside her home to greet her. Every minute people were barging through the doors. She avoided the crowd. Shivani tried to remain calm and focus on the seriousness and sacredness of the ceremony and the new life she was about to embark on.

Many of her extended family members attended the wedding. This was memorable because Sharmela and Sunil had not been reunited with their family for quite some time. Family from the Cayman Islands, Minnesota, New York, Virginia, Canada, and Florida were in attendance.

Traditionally, when the groom arrives at the bride's home, he has to be greeted by the bride's family upon entering. There are rituals that need to be performed before he enters the home. He takes his place by the priest, in the same spot where the couple will take their vows.

After two and a half hours of getting ready, the moment had finally arrived. Shivani peeked through her bedroom window and saw her husband and his family. Minutes later, she was escorted to the backyard wedding ceremony in her mother's arms.

Shivani's guests assembled around the "marrow," a sacred arch made out of branches, under which the bride and groom remain for the duration of the ceremony. Shivani was forbidden to look at her guests because Hindu tradition teaches that it is bad luck to do so. The only person she was allowed to look at was Kevin. He looked handsome, and nervous also. He said to Shivani, "You look beautiful. I love you." Shivani was happy to block everyone out except her husband. Their happiness was most important.

The ceremony represented her parents fulfilling their last parental rites and allowing Shivani's husband to assume her care. Under a white linen sheet, Kevin then placed "sindoor" on Shivani's forehead, which is a red powdery substance that symbolize a woman's married status, and the couple took their seven step vows.

When the ceremony concluded, everyone proceeded to the reception venue. Shivani then focused on making everyone feel as comfortable as possible.

Sunil and Sharmela were the host and hostess of this event and tried to give their daughter the best in life. Sunil had always told her that she made them proud. She was the youngest of three children, and the first to graduate from college with a bachelor's degree.

But Shivani was not at ease. Sharmela looked weary, with tear-filled eyes. Sharmela cried even more as her son Anil recalled going to college with Shivani and their childhood at Nanny's house.

Sharmela's tears were not all about Shivani. She felt partly responsible for forcing her son to attend the same college as Shivani. Anil had been accepted to Ivy League colleges in New Jersey, but Sharmela wanted her children to attend the same college so that Anil could keep a watchful eye over Shivani. Sharmela had felt certain that he would be able to take care of his younger sister and not allow her to be taken advantage of.

Shivani's father also looked unhappy and tired—Shivani did not know why.

Shivani soon became annoyed and unhappy. Here she was, attempting to enjoy herself when her parents were not. She could only focus her attention on making her parents and others joyous on this occasion.

As the night came to a close, everyone merged together as one big family and began to celebrate with the newlyweds. The couple was happy to see this. Earlier in the celebration, Shivani's family and Kevin's family had stayed on different sides of the room.

Shivani and Kevin ventured off on their honeymoon the following Monday. She was excited about starting their journey together and could not wait to spend time alone with Kevin. They decided to keep it local, only traveling as far as Atlantic City for three days. Shivani's sister Seeta and brother-in-law Suresh had made a three days, two nights reservation for them at a Hyatt Hotel in central New Jersey. The newlyweds stayed at the Hyatt over the weekend and then went to the Taj Mahal on Monday.

The couple spend the remainder of their time at the Taj Mahal Casino Resort.

Though excited about their honeymoon, Shivani was annoyed about Kevin being on the phone the entire time. She was really puzzled by that. Shivani even sought guidance from a psychic when they were in Atlantic City. The psychic advised her that someone had cast an evil spell on her. The psychic also warned that Kevin's hands were tied by a family member brainwashing him to leave the relationship. She warned Kevin that he would want to leave. "You wanted a good girl," the psychic told him. "Now you have a good wife, so don't leave."

Kevin clearly had forgotten about those words. Shivani was not happy with the reading, so she decided to take matters into her own hands. She did everything in her power to make sure her husband stayed with her.

But Kevin suspicious behavior on their honeymoon was just a preview of behaviors Shivani had to endure for the next couple of months. Things quickly changed after the wedding. Shivani noticed certain odd behaviors from Kevin, from confusion to indecision and a need to constantly rely on family members to make decisions for him.

Shivani thought that these things were strange, but she hoped it was because they were just beginning to spend time alone, especially overnight for the first time, and he was shy.

From the beginning, Kevin's lifestyle was also dissimilar to hers. Kevin liked the fast life, while Shivani was more introverted. But she figured things would work out, since they were both individuals who could compromise and adapt to any solution that was best suited for them. That belief quickly changed after they tied the knot.

Shivani was wrong. When things were not going well, Kevin would run away from reality and seek a new beginning, thinking that making a fresh start would heal his pain rather than making his present situation better. Kevin never finished what he started, which is contrary to what he had said he believed.

Shivani's concerns about Kevin's behavior began a while back. Kevin and Shivani had had phone conversations on a regular basis, with Kevin visiting her on weekends. Their long-distance engagement seemed to work out well, with the exception of phone calls he would receive from a certain female. Kevin usually shut his phone off when he came to visit Shivani, behavior she found strange in the man she was set to marry. He said his reason for doing it was to designate all of his attention for her. But Shivani had busted him on one occasion when he received a text message from a female expressing her concerns about his whereabouts.

Another incident had taken place while Kevin was spending a weekend at Shivani's home. He missed two phone calls with blocked caller ID. Shivani picked up the phone on the third call, and the caller was a female. Shivani said, "Kevin is playing games with you. He told me that he had broken up with you." As it happened, Kevin had already attempted to cover his own tracks by using this line on Shivani. He insisted that he had ended the relationship with "that" female prior to the engagement.

In subsequent days, Shivani called Kevin's family to inquire what was going on. They advised her not to tell her family about the situation; Kevin's family would take care of matters. Obviously, however, nothing was taken care of, since Shivani received another call from the same female saying that she was still with Kevin.

Shivani eventually became furious that she was receiving calls from this female. When she questioned the calls, Kevin got very defensive and raised his voice and hands as if to hit her. Kevin even went so far as to break his cell phone.

Shivani had reflected on these incidents before the wedding. She realized that they were signs of unfaithfulness, but she had not taken heed. The phone calls were not all, either. Kevin was never at home when he said he was, or at his job when he claimed to be working overtime. One of his family members admitted that Kevin's paychecks were usually short, and the hours he claimed to have worked were not reflected on his paystubs.

In the midst of getting engaged Kevin contacted Shivani, and convey some thoughts of moving to New Jersey permanently. His family assumed that he wanted to do this to be closer to Shivani, because he seemed very sad and lonely. According to Sharda, she and her husband wanted Kevin to take some responsibility and live on his own.

Shivani's family was not thrilled about this because they wanted Kevin and Shivani to be married first. Shivani's parents told Kevin that he needed to find a job before he could move. It was not long before Kevin was able to locate a job and he moved to New Jersey.

Kevin's controlling behavior toward Shivani started when he moved to New Jersey. Every time Shivani and Kevin would get into arguments, he would leave and return hours later. Shivani was worried sick about this habit of his. Kevin seemed to be a ticking time bomb waiting to explode. He had a lot of built-up anger, fear, and regret in his life, which Shivani later realized was what caused him to be unstable.

Shivani saw in Kevin the clear signs of a possessive man, but what could she do about it? Arrangements had already been made and the wedding was going to proceed. Shivani's family had initially arranged for the wedding to take place after she would be finished with her master's degree. Kevin's move to New Jersey put Shivani's education in limbo and caused her wedding to be earlier than her family had planned.

In the meantime, Shivani had to keep secrets from family and friends the reign Kevin already had over her life. It started with mental abuse, similar to any abusive relationship. He would control her time on the phone and would always inquire about who she was speaking to. Shivani's phone was replaced nine times and Kevin's phone was replaced twice, since breaking cell phones seemed to be one of his favorite hobbies. Shivani had no personal space in her life even during the engagement.

Fast forward to the days following their honeymoon. Shivani's purity eventually became a nuisance for her husband. This was very confusing to her: what else could a man ask for? Shivani was chaste at the time of her marriage and was very inexperienced. Shivani thought her husband would appreciate this rose garden she had to offer to him— this priceless gift. Instead, her inexperience infuriated him. Kevin stated that he was not sexually satisfied, so three days after their honeymoon, he kicked and slapped Shivani violently about the head for several minutes. Although there were times that Shivani vocally protested her desire of not engaging into any sexual activities with him, Kevin ignored her requests and continued to force himself on her. Kevin's abusive behavior toward Shivani continued. He would drag her on the floor by her hair and began to choke her until she lost consciousness, all the while screaming and threatening more violence. Shivani was confused because she had always thought a woman's purity was valuable. This was what her parents had instilled in her. Now she was being beaten because of her naiveté.

Every day was becoming a dreadful battle for Shivani to fight. She feared her life was falling apart, and she could not identify the problem so it could be fixed. It felt as though she was living in a home where she knew her roof was leaking because she could feel it, but she could not find the source of the leak.

The abuse continued. Kevin incorporated degrading words like "bitch" into his mental and physical abuse, especially when Shivani did not agree with the decisions or plans Kevin made for their future. One day after getting into an argument, Kevin began to slap her on the head and broke her glasses. There were plenty of other instances when Kevin struck, kicked, choked, and spat out murder threats at her.

The couple's main topic of contention was traveling to his family home in Brooklyn. Kevin had close ties with his family. His brother Marcus was the person who took all responsibility for Kevin's welfare. Kevin explained to Shivani about his family life and upbringing in Guyana. He went even further by adding that his family was poverty-stricken. Kevin was the main source of financial support for his parents because he was unmarried and did not had as much responsibility as his siblings did. However, he conveniently forgot to mention this fact before the wedding.

Shivani had no objection to Kevin's obligations, but she thought it would have been polite to be told about them prior to marriage. Knowing the information probably would not have made a difference, but it would have helped Shivani to understand Kevin's strange allegiance to his family.

Kevin's parents had moved to the United States shortly before the wedding. After the couple's wedding, they frequently traveled to Brooklyn to visit Shivani's in-laws. During this time, Kevin told Shivani that a cousin he was close to was sick and in a hospital on Long Island, New York. Every weekend, Kevin and Shivani would commute to the Bronx and spend both days there. The commute had become very demanding and expensive, but because Kevin had promised to make the visits, the couple had no choice but to go. They never had a single weekend to themselves.

As time progressed, the illness took its toll on Kevin's cousin, and it became time to make funeral arrangements. Everyone was trying to figure out what contributions should be made if Kevin's cousin passed away. Kevin wanted to contribute two thousand dollars toward the funeral. Shivani pointed out to him that they had just gotten married and could not afford to accumulate such a large sum on short notice. They still had outstanding credit card payments to make for their wedding expenses. This dispute created a lot of chaos.

In the midst of dealing with Kevin's family issues, Shivani found out that she was pregnant on October 25, 2005. This was definitely not good timing because of the constant disagreements, financial constraints, abuse and insecurities, it would only be wise to abort the offspring.

The couple had just gotten married, was already having problems, and was in no position to welcome an offspring. Shivani, in a fragile state of mind, was stressed and not sure what decision to make. Terminating the pregnancy may have sounded appealing, but Shivani's culture forbade that act. Only a life-threatening condition could be allowed to prevent her from carrying the baby to term.

As soon as she learned of the pregnancy, Shivani contacted Kevin. He appeased her over the phone by saying they would talk about it when he returned home. Shivani felt relieved because she needed that comfort. But once Kevin got home, he began screaming at her. Then he forced alcohol down Shivani's throat in an attempt to induce a miscarriage. He flung her against the bed while threatening to yank "it" out of her. This was a turning point for Shivani, when she began to truly fear for her life.

Eventually, in November 2005, Kevin left for a week to attend his cousin's funeral. Prior to his departure, Shivani committed the ultimate act of sin according to her religion. She had mixed feelings about it. Kevin made the final decision to abort the fetus. Even at such a moment, Shivani still felt she had no control over her life or body. Her heart told her to stay true to her husband's will, even though she knew about the consequences that could result from this life-changing decision.

Shivani's doctors explained there would be some abdominal discomfort, nausea, and a risk that surgery could be needed if complications occurred. Before she knew it, the release forms were signed, the show was over, and everyone resumed their true characters.

Kevin started to distance himself from Shivani, and retained his paychecks so he could contribute to his cousin's funeral. He missed work without mentioning it to Shivani. When he returned to New Jersey, he said that he needed to have a separate savings account from the joint account they shared, and that he needed to put his valuable items in the bank for security.

Kevin traveled between Brooklyn and New Jersey for couple of weeks, and ultimately the couple was separated for three months. Shivani attempted to talk to Kevin's mother about the problems they were experiencing, but Kevin's mother terminate all phone calls, claiming the phone battery had died.

In the past, Shivani's mother-in-law had advised Shivani to understand Kevin. She explained that individuals born from the Scorpion planet in the month of October, as Kevin was, tended to have a temper and to behave in a violent manner. She gave the example of one of her neighbors in Guyana, Shaun, a boy in his twenties. He was born under the same Scorpion planet, and almost every day he would physically abuse his wife, giving her bruises and bodily injuries.

Shivani then realized her mother-in-law was justifying Kevin's behavior; she wasn't going to help Shivani resolve their problems. Shivani tried desperately to make her mother-in-law recognize that Kevin had a real anger problem. The woman responded, "Men treat women like animals. A wife needs to satisfy her husband in every way possible so that he does not chase after other women."

Plainly, Shivani was not going to receive any assistance from Kevin's family. She continued being submissive to her husband. By that point, Shivani's situation had become unbearable for her to handle alone. She needed a shoulder to lean on and some direction.

One of the many people she could have sought advice from was her cousin Dan. But she knew she could not go to Dan. Two months into the relationship, Dan had called and warned her to break it off because he had some suspicions about the dark secrets Kevin was hiding. Shivani became more cautious, but she did not break the engagement off. Who knows what might have been the outcome if Dan had shared his suspicions with Shivani's parents?

When Kevin stayed in New Jersey, Shivani was devastated that he was gone. She grieved and cried. Although he treated her badly, she still wanted her marriage to work.

During Kevin's absence, Shivani's cousin Racheal was in the hospital going through chemotherapy and a bone marrow transplant. Shivani would call Racheal and they would talk for hours over the phone. Shivani spoke to her every day—they were close confidants. Racheal shared her own problems as well. They were both two unhappy people at that point in their lives, and all they had was each other for comfort.

Racheal advised, "Shivani, go down on bended knees to Maha Kali, goddess of dissolution and destruction, with your tears and problems, just like you come to me, and she will help you."

One morning, Racheal went in for surgery, and the end result was not successful. Shivani had not realized how serious Racheal's illness was. While Shivani was at work in January 2006, she received a phone call from her cousin Dan that Racheal had passed away. When Shivani found out, a part of her was broken. She was in shock.

Shivani immediately left work. She could not focus. The love and attachment Shivani had developed for Racheal over this short period of time was immense. Racheal had worked tirelessly at Shivani's wedding, baking a black cake and making last-minute preparations. Shivani felt trapped, her support system was no longer in existence. Her husband had abandoned her, her cousin had passed away, and she had no one to turn to for guidance.

Shivani surrendered herself to God, as Rachael had advised during their last phone conversation. She fasted until the day Kevin returned.

In Shivani's culture, wedding vows were not taken lightly, especially by the women in her family. Shivani's aunt Mary said, "Honey, you need to do whatever your heart tells you. I stuck with my husband because of my reputation and my children. I had a daughter, and I did not want her husband to look down on her because her parents were separated."

So Shivani let her heart take the lead. Shivani's heart badly wanted her marriage to last.

During their separation, her communication with Kevin was minimal. Shivani's family was not happy with the choices Kevin made to neglect her, nor about the abortion and the monetary contributions he made without her consent. On the other hand, Kevin's family felt he had an obligation to spend the week in the Bronx for the funeral. The discord between Kevin's and Shivani's families put additional strain on the marriage, and things fell apart.

Traditionally within Indo-Guyanese arranged marriages, when there is a problem between the bride and groom, the first step is to seek spiritual guidance from a family priest. The priest advises both parties either to fast strictly, meaning to abstain from meat, fish, and dairy products, or to do meditations to the Goddess for peace and stability in the relationship. After these actions are completed, the couple returns to the matchmakers—the people who were involved in pairing the couple. In most cases, it's the parents or guardians of the couple. They all hold a meeting to discuss their problems and work toward possible solutions.

Prior to Shivani's separation from Kevin, the families' rapport had become nonexistent, so consulting with a priest or meeting to discuss issues were not options. Attempting to stabilize the couple's marriage would have worked only if both parties were willing.

The holidays came around, and Shivani and Kevin could not enjoy their first Christmas together as a married couple since they were separated at the time. So they made arrangements to meet up for lunch and a movie.

Their meeting was kept secret from their families because the families were at war, and at this point, Kevin and Shivani were not ready to risk losing the trust of their families. Shivani was surprised to see Kevin making even this much sacrifice, since he had made minimal sacrifices during their marriage so far.

For her part, although Shivani was a married woman, she was afraid to disobey her parents' wish that she avoid Kevin. By this time, Shivani's parents were well aware of Kevin's controlling behavior and other strange actions, based on what they had seen since he came to live in New Jersey.

While Kevin was gone, the couple maintained telephone communication with each other. Kevin agreed that he would move back to New Jersey the couple had mend their matters and disagreement. Shivani made arrangements to secure a new living arrangement. In fact,

Once Shivani knew that she and Kevin were going to give the marriage a second shot, she stepped out on faith and picked up her husband from his brother's residence on February third. They were both ecstatic to see each other, and their transition from separated to reunited went well during the first week. The couple put equal effort into decorating their condo. Although there were days when the burden was too overwhelming for Shivani to withstand singlehandedly, she was always optimistic. She thought that the time spent apart would make their hearts grow fonder of one another, and perhaps make Kevin realize there was still some hope for their relationship to work out.

However, Kevin sure had a funny way of shifting Shivani's views around. They finally had their own place of residence, and Shivani was quite sure Kevin was happy about that. No watchful eyes. No interruptions. Just "Shivani, I am your husband, and you do as I say." The initial problems that had created the separation quickly crept back into their lives, and this time it destroyed the connection they had. Shivani realized that Kevin had not and would not change, no matter how hard she tried to give him the opportunity to reflect and see how much he was hurting her. He continued to abuse, mistreat, and control her.

The couple argued almost every weekend after Kevin's return home. Now money became a major issue in their relationship. Allegedly, during the separation, Kevin had found a job working as a subcontracted construction worker. Unbeknownst to Shivani, however, he had been terminated because of dishonesty. Shivani was paying all of the bills, and neither Kevin nor his family cared as long as their needs were satisfied. With hindsight, Shivani suspected that Kevin already had that goal in mind before the marriage. She was an easy target to help him ease his financial obligations. After marriage , Kevin had advised Shivani that he had promised to fulfill monetary obligations toward his family. His initial plan had been to accumulate the required funds prior to moving to New Jersey, but that had not happened. After the wedding, Kevin and Shivani had to work diligently to accumulate the promised funds, unbeknownst to her parents.

Shivani had exhausted all her options to make their marriage succeed, but to her disappointment, things were not working out in her favor. Kevin depended on Shivani desperately for financial stability and for his legal status, because he was not authorized to work in the United States. Shivani had to bear the burden. That led Shivani to cut corners to ensure *all* their financial obligations were met. " He overdrawn her accounts to satisfy his obligations, leaving her with unauthorized payments to tend to.

Shivani (going through their closets and coming upon roller skates):
    Kevin, where did these come from?

Kevin: Hey, give me those! They're mine, and why are you going through the stuff in my closet space?

Shivani: I am not "going through" your stuff, I was cleaning up your side of the space because all your clothes are on the floor and the closet doors cannot shut. When did you go shopping?

Kevin: Since when you do you clean? It was last week—I had free time at work, so I went over to the mall and bought a pair. They were on sale …

Shivani: Ha ha, funny … Kevin, you do realize we have bills to pay and outstanding credit card payments? You need to stop spending money carelessly, especially on roller skates. When are you going to have time for this? And since when did skating become a hobby for you? You need to grow up and stop behaving like a kid in a candy store! Everything you see, you buy. You did that same s**t last week when you went to Radio Shack to buy batteries and somehow bought games for your PS2 instead, which threw us totally out of our budget for this week. Now our mortgage payment is going to be a month late!

By this point in the conversation, Kevin was gnashing his teeth and Shivani could imagine steam coming out of his ears. Rage was overtaking his body, and that was her signal to get out of the way before Kevin began his customary manic behavior,

Shivani quickly exited the room to allow Kevin some space and time to cool down.

When Kevin and Shivani were separated, he had affairs with other women. Shivani found out he had cheated on her with a woman named Samantha. He claimed it was a "friendly" relationship. To add insult to injury, he spread rumors about the newlyweds' sex life to his family and friends in the Bronx.

Kevin became even more jealous and controlling once the couple reunited. Kevin began to isolate Shivani from her family. He also agreed to isolate himself from his family, but he never did. If Shivani returned from work late because of traffic, he would accuse her of being at her parents' house or cheating on him with a coworker. He knew that if his abuse continued, there could be extreme consequences, even imprisonment. He feared that if Shivani's parents were being informed about his behavior, those consequences would come to pass, because her parents were very protective of her.

Kevin ridiculed Shivani with words, saying that she was "nothing" and that she was just useless. He manipulated her into thinking that she had a problem when it was really him. He blamed Sharmela for the couple's separation.

Sharmela felt that Kevin was wrong for abandoning Shivani during her pregnancy and jeopardizing her safety with an abortion. She felt that Kevin should not have taken matters so lightly. Kevin became upset at Shivani's mom for addressing the situation. He did not take responsibility for his actions; instead, he blamed everything on everyone except himself. Especially after he abused Shivani, he would tell her that she made him do it, and that he had never been like this before he met her.

Kevin and Shivani drove to his family's house in Brooklyn one Saturday afternoon shortly after their reunion. The couple had gotten into an argument en route because Shivani told him she knew that he had not been faithful, and she had all the evidence. Family and close friends had told her about his infidelities, so she had begun secretly recording his phone conversations.

Kevin was not happy to hear this. His body became visibly filled with rage. He threatened to steer the car off the Verrazano Narrows Bridge. This is a narrow, double-decker bridge suspended over the Hudson River, connecting Staten Island to Brooklyn. Shivani was driving the car in the far-right lane. Kevin reached over from the passenger seat to turn the steering wheel toward him. Shivani began to scream hysterically. As she panicked, she could only cry out, "Stop!"

Kevin said to her, "We will both die together."

Her body trembled, perspiration poured out of her soul, and it felt like her heart was beating a hundred times a minute. Kevin then had the nerve to yell out for Shivani to calm down. Shivani knew God was on her side that day because, even though she was near death, she stayed alert enough to roll down her window. The drivers in the other lanes were looking at her silver Hyundai Elantra as it wobbled, and thankfully there was a police car three lanes over. After noticing the police, Kevin became calm, because he was always cautious whenever it came to law enforcement officials.

Kevin remained quiet until they arrived at his family's home in Brooklyn. He got out of the car and Shivani immediately left. This was another turning point when she knew she needed to get out of this "fairy tale" life. She realized that she needed an exit strategy.

In April 2006, Kevin and Shivani were in the kitchen making dinner. He usually made the main course, a curry, and Shivani would make the rice and other side dishes.

While cooking, they began to discuss their plans for the following weekend. He wanted them to go to Brooklyn, and she refused. They started to argue again. Kevin then threatened to harm her. He grabbed a pair of scissors and attempted to slash her throat.

Fearing for her life, Shivani tried to call 911. Kevin then violently shoved her to the ground and tore the phone cord from the wall, forcing her to terminate the phone call before she could ask the operator for assistance. He then wrapped the phone cord around her neck and began choking Shivani, depriving her of oxygen and saying, "Let me see who you're going to call now."

After he had strangled her for several minutes, the police arrived. He quickly locked her in the bedroom. Once he finally opened the front door, the police began to question him. Kevin lied and said that no one had called 911. The cops asked if everything was okay. Then he told the cops he had meant to dial 411 and dialed 911 by accident.

Kevin did not allow Shivani to come out of the bedroom because he would have been arrested if the cops had seen or had any inkling that she was being abused. Kevin was residing illegally in the United States, and an arrest could prevent his legalization papers from being processed. Shivani had to deny the fact that she had called the cops to Kevin and state that the neighbors probably did it.

After the cops left, Kevin entered the bedroom as if nothing had happened. Several minutes passed before Shivani finally went back into the kitchen. She could have ended it all right in that moment. All of the pieces were in place—police protection plus Kevin's arrest equaled a free woman! It was a perfect opportunity to get out of her marriage, but fear and shame clouded her judgment.

Shivani and Kevin got into another huge argument a week later. This had become a common thing for them. Kevin slapped and dragged Shivani into the bedroom so the neighbors would not hear. Kevin shut the doors and then jumped on top of her and choked her while she gasped for air. After he released her, she ran as quickly as she could to the telephone and he ran for a weapon. He picked up closest thing he could put his hands on, which happened to be the same pair of scissors from their last battle.

As Shivani frantically tried to get to the phone, she was frozen dead in her tracks when he began to brutally slash himself on the arm. Blood gushed onto the hardwood floor. He rushed toward the front door to exit their home. Just before he left, he turned to her and said, "I'm going to tell the cops you did this to me." And he left.

Shivani was terrified and astonished about what had just transpired. How could he be so cruel as to place false allegations on her? She feared what this man was capable of, so she hurried to call her parents and tell them what was going on. Within two minutes, Kevin was at the door again, asking her to let him in with tears in his eyes.

At first, she hesitated out of fear, but she did it. Her family did make a call to 911. However, when law enforcement arrived, the couple did not answer the door.

After this incident, Kevin made repeated threats to hunt down and kill Shivani and her family if they ever reported his abuse to the police. On many occasions, Kevin even sexually forced himself upon her, despite her vocal protests and physical attempts to resist.

Kevin clearly was not stable. It took Shivani a very long time to realize this. He had no control over his life. He was a puppet and his family held the strings, even though he was a grown man and had a wife. Nothing pleased him. Kevin took all his anger and frustration out on Shivani. If he did not have a good job, it was Shivani's fault. If he did not get his naturalization paperwork completed, it was her fault because she did not get a good lawyer and made him waste a lot of money. If she took him to the doctor, he said she was trying to make him more ill.

Nothing Shivani did for him was meant to earn her praise, but rather to elevate him so at least they could be on the same level. She attempted to enroll him at Lincoln Tech, since he had expressed an interest in taking up a trade. He said that he would get the books to study, but he never took the initiative to do so. Kevin was like a child. He had to be reminded to do something or else he would forget.

Even Kevin's parents made Shivani a scapegoat for his problems. But Shivani did not destroy him. Kevin was the one who tried to make himself a better person with books like *How to Change Your Life with Witchcraft*, which Shivani found in her husband's closet, buried under his clothes. Shivani did not know much about how supernatural power worked, but she knew it was no joke. Kevin must have been carrying the book with him everywhere if it been kept hidden from her.

When she confronted Kevin about the book, he threaten to chop off her fingers. He stated this book had been in his family for generations, and he stole it from his grandfather. After this, Kevin became even more terrified.

Shivani was never happy with him, but she tried desperately to preserve the marriage because of her religious beliefs. She repressed all her angry thoughts and moved on. She was warned by her mother, who said, "Honey, this is not for you." Shivani chose not to listen, even when her mother said, "You will get hurt."

Shivani's family disapproved of her decision to move into the condo with Kevin after he had abandoned her for three months. Shivani asked Shamela if she would accept her back into her home if she gets hurt. Sharmela said, "I support you 100 percent, but don't forget Mommy has warned you. You deserve better and need to be treated like the princess and gem you have become. Never settle for less than you deserve."

Shivani asked, "Mom, how could I leave him? What will family and friends think? How will society see me?"

"Shivani, I gave birth to you. No one knows your story like I do. Frankly, it is not their business. You are my child, and I am concerned about your welfare. I have given him my youngest daughter, and you were innocent. He has taken away that precious gift from you, and I will not let him drag you around. Let him go. If he desperately wants you back, then he will return in the same hurried fashion that he left. If he does not, then you need to move on. You will find happiness and someone who will respect and value you for what you are worth. Mommy will always be the guiding light in your life, and when she goes to heaven, she will shower you with her blessings. Don't ever be afraid or worried, my child."

Shivani said, "Mommy, I am scared. How do I make this transition?"

Reaching out, Sharmela said, "My child, come here. You are Devi, Goddess. You continue to serve the gods, and they will continue to shower their bountiful blessings. Have faith."

Shivani had seen the good and bad characteristics of her husband, but chose to stick it out until the end. She truly thought that she could change him for the better. That belief finally died when she came home from work one Saturday afternoon in June. She opened the door to their apartment and a moldy smell struck her. She began to look around the apartment, calling out, "Honey, where are you?"

Laundry was emptied on the floor. The deep yellow piggy bank was on the computer desk, and now held only pennies. She had given it to him earlier in the day filled with quarters to do laundry. The sofa was filled with clothing belonging to her. His pictures were gone. In the bedroom, clothes were everywhere and items were scattered on the floor. Her suitcase was gone.

As she left the bedroom, she noticed there was a note on dining room table, written on a yellow notepad. As she began to read it, her knees became weak and her body began to shake as though she was having a panic attack. It said:

Dear Sweet Mama,

You know things can't work between us. You don't like when my family calls and I don't have a job. I have decided to leave. Take care and I know you will make it far because you have the determination. I don't know what my life will turn out to be yet. You were good to me!

Over the previous week, Kevin had been extra vigilant about her work schedule. He had also wanted to know the whereabouts of their marriage certificate and income tax returns. She had thought it was strange for him to inquire about those documents, but then she quickly cleared all negative thoughts out of her head and stayed optimistic.

The night before Kevin left, he had received a phone call from a family member between eleven o'clock and twelve o'clock at night. Initially, she thought it was odd that his family would call at that time of night. Kevin assured her that it was nothing important. The next morning, he woke Shivani up at six o'clock to offer prayers to the celestial at a lake in New Brunswick.

As Shivani had left for work, he walked her to the car and gave her a passionate kiss. He even volunteered to have the laundry done and lunch cooked before she returned home. She said quietly, "Wow, this is a new man overnight," not knowing his intentions.

Now, her heart skipped a beat. She felt an instant rush of relief! It was like a weight had lifted off her shoulders. She was not angry or sad as she once would have been when he left. Strangely, her conscience was free, knowing that she was not the one to leave the marriage. She was even more ready to embark on a life free from the physical and emotional pain that he had inflicted upon her.

Shivani's feet raced out the door and toward her car. Her destination: the place where it all began—her parents' house.

Upon arriving at their home, her mom embraced her even before she entered the door. Sharmela knew Kevin had left because Shivani's sister had seen Kevin at the nearby shopping area. She had assumed Kevin was waiting for someone to pick him up, since he had a suitcase in his hand. A van drove up. As she began to approach the van, he was already inside the vehicle, and they drove off.

Shivani's heart filled with disappointment knowing that the life she envisioned had turned into a complete disaster. Her mind could not help but wonder why God had turned his back on her and given her the opposite of what she requested.

Kevin had kept her in fear for her life. He used threatening looks and gestures for intimidation. The verbal threats would chop her spirit into a million pieces and flush it down the toilet. He would monitor her telephone calls, putting all calls on speaker so he could hear her conversations. He constantly threatened to kill her and to commit suicide as well. A favorite saying of his was, "If I kill myself, you will take another man, so I will kill you and then myself."

Poem on life
There is the possibility that she could get hurt,
betrayed and even ruin her reputation.
A woman's character is priceless in her
culture. Life is unpredictable.
Even with the possibility of being caught
into the web of disappointment,
she ventured into this realm of reality, taking
her chances, knowing very well that she could
be bitten by the serpent of hurt that is real and
ready to strike. It is not unnatural to have desires.

It is that very persistence and desire that molds the nature of our minds and fulfills the desires we seek.

With all its trials and tribulations, Shivani knew that assuming the title of "wife" was a serious responsibility. She had had a great desire since childhood to be a faithful and loving wife. So her desires came true. Shivani was betrothed within two months of her first meeting with a man, and was a married woman eight months later. Even though she still didn't know him well enough, the thought of this new adventure made her ecstatic.

The very day after her boat sailed into the harbor of her husband, his iron-clad hook took hold as he began to mold her into what he desired her to be. Accepting her as she was was never an option. He wanted things his way or, as she would soon find out, there would be dire consequences. She was horrified to discover that the love she effortlessly bestowed upon him would never be reciprocated. Her goal was to please him; his was to make her a slave to him.

Her heart was his, but his was not hers. His heart was filled with wild thoughts of fornication and deceit. Her heart was dedicated to being the wife he supposedly wanted while honoring, loving, and cherishing him; his was dedicated to mentally and physically abusing her. Shivani's desires were to start a family and give him the happiness he supposedly wanted; his desires were cruelty and betrayal. Her desire was to stick with the vows she had made, for better or worse; his was only to make her life a living hell and disappear. He took her soul hostage.

Shivani's body ached with the pain he inflicted upon her. Yet, she always managed to seize the opportunity to massage and soothe his pain. While tears streamed down her face, he never comforted her. But her shoulders were always there when he needed someone to lean on. He destroyed her life, used her, and damaged relationships she had with the friends and relatives who stood by her when she needed them the most. Each prayer she made to the Lord was to unite the two of them so that they might live in happiness. Never was she allowed peace and serenity at any moment with him.

Chapter 4

LIFE AFTER:
COPING MECHANISMS

Shivani opened her diary and saw a poem she
had written during her teenage years:

*   *   *

*Truthful and sweet, my husband is quick
wit, funny, and industrious too.*

To whom my strong desires and solemn trust given.

Behold, I am a woman of strong desire to please and wish upon the star.

I know that he has that desire to please me too.

*I wish upon the stars that his hand is gentle upon
me and cherish every moment we spend.*

*I wish upon stars that his love surpass my expectation
and one that is magical and sweet.*

*I wish upon the stars that my heart never feels lonely and
my eyes never weary from the tears of hurt or pain.*

*I wish upon the stars that he does not leave the burden
of the home upon me and take me for granted.*

*I wish upon the stars that his words only speak the sweet
nectar of love and not that of insults or pain.*

*I wish upon the stars that he does not lay his hand on me to
inflict hurt but that of only pleasure and guidance.*

Sometimes we forget the value of family. Life experiences force us to recognize the true bond that exists between family members, especially the mother and daughter bond. Shivani's mother's eyes were filled with tears and her heart saddened by her daughter's ordeal, for which she felt responsible. Shivani's eyes could not help but be washed over by tears, too, like rain on a car windshield.

It was actually the first time ever that her parents set foot in the home they had bought for Shivani and her husband. They had been prohibited by Kevin from visiting Shivani. Shivani had agreed with this decision because she did not want any problems within her marriage. Kevin made it clear before he returned home after their separation that he did not want her parents to come to their home and intervene in their lives. Shivani's parents had respected her wishes and stayed out of her home and out of the couple's life.

Shivani's father and brother began to clean up, throwing away Kevin's belongings. Shivani's eyes filled with tears, knowing that all the effort she had put into this marriage was for nothing. Her weaknesses were exposed for all to see now. She had lost self-confidence and put her faith in love and culture.

As she was cleaning, she stumbled upon her diary. The diary was not filled with many entries, but some were appropriate for the moment:

Dear Diary,

My eyes are tearing and my soul refuses to come to grips with what is happening. I keep hearing that I am at fault. He keeps blaming my relationship with my parents as the reason for our arguments. I have kept away from my parents because I was hoping he would change. He has not. He has continued to speak ill things toward me. He has continued being violent toward me. I refuse to believe that he does not love me. But one thing is clear, you cannot change a person. Once they have hit you, they will continue to do so.

Shivani's brother Anil told her that guys will test boundaries and see how far they can get with a girl. If they have gotten away with past violence without severe penalty, they will continue the violence, take her for granted, and try to go beyond that. This is what Kevin did; he failed the test miserably.

Shivani was battered and emotionally scarred. She only stayed in the marriage because of the promise she had made to God, her parents, Kevin, and his mother. The vows she took before God on her wedding day gave her assurance that her marriage would work no matter what it took, as long as beforehand she preserved her reputation, her promise to her parents that she would remain a virgin until she got married.

She was promised a lifetime partner who would be her reward for being faithful to her culture. Unfortunately, she stumbled upon an opportunist, one who could easily deceive people with his simple looks and genuine demeanor.

When life is overwhelming and all options seem to have been exhausted, one's mind quickly turns to faith. It was the strong devotion of Shivani's mother that kept Shivani afloat. Sharmela understood her angst because Sharmela's life had not been rosy as Shivani may have thought.

Sharmela never felt her parents' love. Her marriage to Shivani's father was one of content and understanding, Sunil took her as she was—poverty-stricken and unloved.

Sharmela turned to faith in her darkest moments, and through faith, she was able to provide love and strength to her family. It was through her faith that the family was able to overcome life's challenges. When situations become unbearable, she called on God and kept chanting her favorite motto, "Where there is a will, there is a way."

Shivani was never hungry once she returned home. She was provided for luxuriously in her parent's home. She continued to focus her attention on the Lord, whom she believed would fulfill all her dreams and aspirations.

As Shivani put her energy into prayers, her belief became stronger and her mind was totally occupied by duty and devotion. She forgot the problems that she had faced.

When her body was at rest, however, her mind would almost always wonder about Kevin. She would quickly try to forget and think instead of the future and how she would make it.

Her brother wrote a poem when he visited the family home one evening:

"My mind angers at the thought of someone harming or injuring an angel, whose heart is soft and tender. My heart pains with the thought of a man whom she loved inflicting pain upon her. My body shook with anger and my tongue was eager to speak, but my dear sister's welfare came into my thought. I do not want to intervene and refrained from doing so. It is as if she is living in a home which is a prison and torture chamber. She [is] afraid to talk to him, and when she does talk to him, he does not respond or shows a temper. How my hands [yearned] to hurt him and make him cry like a child. How my mouth [wanted] to ignite the fire of anger through words and let the fool know that he is a coward and only beats up on women. [He is] too afraid to beat up on me because his ass would be [whooped]."

Lesson learned. No one should ever give too much of themselves or let it be known what their weaknesses or strong beliefs are. In Shivani's case, her beliefs were taken advantage of and made her very vulnerable. She thought she was being vulnerable for the right reasons; she was a married woman devoting her all to her marriage. She made it known to her husband that she strongly believed in Indo-Guyanese culture, especially the notion of relations being only between one man and one woman. There was no way that she would have pursued another man.

Shivani believed that a person marries for good or bad, and she personally did not believe in more than one marriage. There was a stigma in her culture that no man would want a woman who has been married. As crazy as it may sound, it puts girls at a disadvantage and allows them to be dominated, because men know how strongly girls hold onto these beliefs. Shivani believed that Kevin took advantage of this and knew that, no matter what, she was not going to leave the marriage.

Shivani began her journey of healing through her faith. Her marriage had been the most traumatizing experience she had ever encountered in her life. She would not have wished such an experience on her worst enemy. Her life after abuse would not have been triumphant if it had not been for her mother.

After Kevin departed, it was time for Shivani to concentrate on putting her life together. She moved out of the condo the same night Kevin left and sold her furniture and bedroom set within the following days. She made some repairs and attempted to put the condo up for sale. She borrowed money to pay for the mortgage and some bills. Kevin left her in debt because he had put the entire financial burden on her. He told her that everything was in her name, so she was the one who had to worry about it.

Shivani filed a restraining order against Kevin and proceeded to seek legal advice so she could officially obtain a divorce. Filing for divorce was a daunting task. Because her husband did not have legal documentation of entry and a known address, it became a tiring process. It took approximately two years to obtain a divorce decree.

During that time, she also had to revoke her sponsorship of his naturalization. Through his marriage to a legal resident, Kevin was allowed to apply for naturalization and become a legal resident himself. This naturalization paperwork had to be canceled because of the divorce, and Shivani notified the immigration and naturalization agency about the change. She also had to close all joint accounts. It was time for a more proactive *her* to emerge from it all.

Shivani embraced each day positively, knowing that she would achieve her goals. Her father had always encouraged her to work toward her dreams and never let negative people or the past blur her vision for the future. She was hurt and had fallen flat on her face, but she just let her past be a lesson learned. Don't trust anyone who resides in the dark.

Finally able to get some clarity and space to think, Shivani's to-do list for her life became pretty lengthy. She signed up for music lessons and vocal lessons, and took a few dance classes with her friend, Monique. She could remember Kevin tormenting her about her voice and saying that she had an annoying tone; he was blessed with a good singing voice. So the vocal lessons were first on her list.

A change of environment and activities allowed her to relieve some stress and unwind. She attended a few yoga classes and domestic violence group counseling in Somerville, New Jersey. It helped knowing that she was not alone. Women just like her had had the same experiences, and they all shared that common bond. Shivani's domestic violence counselors gave her an opportunity to express her innermost thoughts. They offered a listening ear and helped her to soothe her pain. She was finally given options to assist her with feeling safe. The counseling sessions allowed her to see that women who are not committed to cultural ties experience abuse as well.

Shivani had become extremely timid throughout her marriage, and even though the worst days of her life were over, she still was not able to face reality. During her marriage, her family would call to find out how the newlyweds were doing, and she could not talk to any of them. She felt ashamed, humiliated, and disgraced.

Now, the thought of answering numerous questions about her defunct marriage, starting her life anew, and possibly finding a new love scared her. She avoided family and friends like the plague. How could a woman who had done everything "right" in life deserve this?

Shivani definitely needed support. But the only person she could muster up enough strength to talk to outside of group counseling was her mom.

Her ninety-year-old grandmother feared that her grandchild was hurt and scurried to the phone to check if she was distressed. Nanny's husky voice said, "Are you okay? Are you in distress? Are you happy? If you are not happy, then it's not for you." This was the same grandmother who had abandoned her own daughter, Lilawatie, because Lilawatie had left her husband and unhappy marriage to marry someone else of a different race. Shivani, surprised, avoided continuing this conversation with Nanny because she was aware of Nanny's medical condition and did not want to put any extra burden upon her.

It actually took five years for Shivani to get where she is today, in a position where she is comfortable and back on solid ground. She had to reclaim her confidence and self-worth. She started off with a master plan—the blueprint consisted of blocking everyone out. She chose to concentrate solely on herself. She knew exactly what steps she needed to take to get where she was heading. So she stayed far away from making hasty decisions.

She focused on what was most important to her, which was establishing her finances. It took a year of working two jobs and saving every dime to repay her outstanding debts.

The second year, she focused on building her career and returned to school for her master's degree. Her ultimate goal was to become a teacher. Three months after her husband left, Shivani started working as a substitute teacher at an arts school. She worked her way toward becoming a classroom teacher the following year, then the coordinator of the after-school program.

The third year was spent rebuilding her cultural discipline and offering devotion to God. She invested time in her Mandir.

In the fourth year, Shivani launched her first business venture.

In the fifth year, she continued to work diligently on her career goals, concentrating on educational leadership, and took her business endeavors to another level.

Working with the public on a daily basis gave her the perspective she had not had five years previously. Due to her sheltered upbringing, Shivani had been programmed to believe a certain way and value certain things. She thought that culture and tradition had to be strictly followed every step of the way.

The older she became, the more she began to realize that things could not go back to the way they had been, no matter how hard she tried. What was highly valued during her parents' era, such as a woman's reputation and faithfulness to culture and tradition, were not as important to Shivani's generation. Through being exposed to the world, Shivani realized that people would treat her based on the way she presented herself. If she exuded a lack of confidence, she would be treated with little respect.

Chapter 5

Self-Reflection: In Shivani's Own Words

A mother's nature is directed by the instinct and love that prevails in her heart. Nature has given the gift of love to a feminine being, a love that is incomparable and unconditional. The one who nurtured me in her womb sought the same happiness that I did, and put the same trust I put into the hands of the one who hurt me.

My mother's intentions were good, not evil. There is not one day when I have blamed her for the person she agreed to betroth me to. After all, it was partially my choice, too. I was brought up as a strong woman and was well aware of my rights. But I was caught in a web of lies, control, and manipulation. When I look back, it is strange to see the things that I allowed to occur, and I wonder why I was so afraid to stand up for myself. Maybe I just thought that all relationships start out badly, and that eventually I would receive the fruits of my labor—the fruits of love. But my thinking was wrong, and never again will I allow anyone to manipulate me.

I allowed society and culture to dictate my actions within my arranged marriage. The possibility of being disgraced and humiliated coerced me to stick with my marriage, but I knew the true feelings of my mind, body, and soul. I was worn out from constantly dealing with pain and stress.

It was the strength of my mother that blessed me with insight. It was her strength that pulled me from the ocean where I was drowning. It is on her boat that my weary body lay and bathed in the sun. It is her compassion that brought light and love back into my heart. The trust that escaped me suddenly began to take root in the soil. My tears dropped upon the earth, but with every tear, there was a tree of desire for happiness and prosperity and fulfillment planted.

A book I once read by Charlotte Perkins Gilman called *The Yellow Wallpaper* came to mind. The story was reminiscent of me—how a strong, motivated, and intelligent woman can be transposed into a person who exhibits no self-confidence. I never imagined I would be caught in this trap.

Over time, my coping mechanism had been to become immune to his behavior toward me. My husband took advantage of my vulnerability, innocence, and ignorance that people like him existed in the world. Especially amongst my peers, most people were appalled by my parents' teaching and upbringing. But I still embrace my culture, even though I experienced the worst aspects of an arranged marriage. I saw that situation as a learning experience, and I came out with my dignity intact and head held high.

Most of the disagreements in our marriage were because of my refusal to be completely submissive to my husband. He was unsure of the direction that his life would take, so he tried hard to distort my life's direction. As my mentor, Monica, would tell me, "You do not need a man to validate you. Stand firm for what you believe in."

I decided it was time to live for me. Why should I sit around and mourn over him? I have my whole life ahead of me. I can accomplish my dreams and discover the new, inner me. I am no longer afraid of embarrassment, afraid to sing, dance, or pursue teaching. He instilled all of these fears of failure and ridicule.

I constantly looked for a way out but was unsure of what direction to go. All I wanted was to love and be loved, to have someone to trust and feel safe with. I desperately wanted a family of my own, only to find out my husband did not have the same sentiments. I was filled with disappointment.

Even worse, everything I had pursued and accomplished prior to marriage seemed to be at a standstill once I met him. I put many aspirations on hold to preserve my marriage. Now I was stuck wondering where I would go from here. None of my dreams were fulfilled, and the love my mother had told me would eventually come did not.

Will it ever come? I wanted the happy life my parents have. This life was promised to me if I wed within the realm of arranged marriage. I was told I would be treated with the utmost respect because I was "pure" before marriage. Instead, my husband hated my pureness and physically showed me how much countless times. My family was told during our pre-marriage meetings that I would have a solid support system when I needed marital advice. His family quickly turned their backs on me and I was left alone to fight my battles. I encountered total betrayal even though I carried out my cultural obligations and what was expected of me by my parents and God. I stayed devoted and loyal to my husband even though he was unfaithful and abusive. The sacredness of my wedding vows was nonexistent.

I now know who I am. I do not need a man to scrutinize my character or try to change me. I am a woman who has strong morals, an advanced educational background, and self-made perseverance to achieve my goals. As a twenty-two year old woman, I financially supported an individual who claimed to be a man when really he was financially, mentally, and physically helpless. I wasted two years of my life sacrificing to make things work. I put every single muscle and all of my time into planning a bright future for Kevin. Time lost can never be regained. The time I could have spent investing in my own well-being, I used to treat Kevin as a valuable gem. When a woman goes above and beyond to do things, a little respect and admiration goes a long way. I received nothing but curses and a destroyed quality of life. He was well aware of my values, but he failed to cherish them. He searched for my dark, underlying secrets to justify his actions, but he could not find any. In the end, fabricated and exaggerated reasons were enough to justify him leaving me.

Kevin trashed my personal belongings, emails, and legal documents, but he could not have cared less that his hasty exit would leave me subject to public criticism. But I do believe we will cross paths one day. He will have to repent for the sins he has committed.

There is no forgiveness in my heart. I am finally free. Today, I live to tell my story because of the strong supporters I have, even when I tried to shun them. Without these people, I would not have been able to guide my ship, anchor my life, and arrive safely at shore. I would probably have drowned at sea or been eaten alive by my husband's abusive ways.

When I lacked direction, my mother liberated me from my bondage. She unwearyingly removed each and every visible and invisible scar from my body and set me free to stand on solid ground. I turned to the celestial being and my mother to take me on this journey called Hope.

I was fixated on the past and uncertain about the future. I could not see my silver lining. But my mother showed me the light at the end of the tunnel. She picked me up off the ground where I fell flat on my face and redirected me to the basic principle, "Never lose your faith in God. If you have forgotten all the values I taught you, never forget this one."

When I returned home after the end of my marriage, I could not look at my father and brother in the eyes. I felt that they had lost respect for me. I had been destined to stay with my husband until death did us part, but I was not able to carry out this tradition.

My father was a staunch believer in maintaining traditions. He was very strict with me and my sister growing up, and also played an instrumental role in my arranged marriage to Kevin. I felt that I had let my family down and let my marriage defeat me. I could not help but think what had I done wrong. I would bury my face in my pillow night after night as tears streamed down my face. At times, I would lock myself in my room and did not want to come out.

But my mother could read me like a book and knew exactly what I was feeling without me ever uttering a word. My mother delicately showed me that I could pull through and stand up on my own. She showed me that this was not a defeat but an experience with bountiful opportunity.

I needed to take control of my life so I would not end up being defeated. I had grown up in a family where we never take being defeated lightly. We are fighters, and we are determined to make things happen. We work as a team. So when one member is in pain or experiences grief, the rest of us scurry over to provide comfort and support.

My mom is the driving force that keeps our family enlightened and motivates us to be our greatest, even when we lack strength. So I took my mom's hand, and she led me on the journey of hope.

We encountered many bumps along the way, especially from people who had questions about my choices within the marriage. My mom stood tall, took the giant wind that came my way, and sailed our boat through. She sheltered me beneath her wings.

However, I knew that there would be a time to come out and fight my own battles. I needed to get out of my old character and live my life as a strong, educated, and independent woman. I knew that good things would eventually come my way, but a plan was necessary. My mom had fully equipped me with a life survival kit.

As that chapter in my life came to a close, I was horrified to think that I might not ever move on, live, or love again. Even my mom had her breaking points at times. The burden of spearheading my recovery became overwhelming for my mother to carry. Yet, she held on to me closely, not letting me lose sight of my faith in life and God.

Without guidance, it would have been hard to see the future, since I was fixated on "him." My mom's strength taught me that I needed to embrace one of the essential facts of life. You cannot control the wind, but you have control of the sail. The positive energy that my mom bestowed upon me was all the motivation I needed to carry me through another day. My mother is someone I completely trust, and I had every intention of standing at her side.

Once my inner beliefs changed, I came to realize that these were the choices I had made in my life.

In 2006, when I hit rock bottom, there was no hope. I was fortunate to find a job at the arts school. The arts school gave me relief. The children I worked with were so bright and vibrant that I was no longer able to fixate on the past. The children signified the hope of better tomorrows and that the past would be left behind.

When I entered this brand-new setting, I had nothing to offer but a good heart and the mindset to educate and provide supervision for these beautiful children. I was introduced to a different aspect of life. I was fascinated by these children's talents, giving them encouragement here and there. I was still helpless, yet here I was motivating children.

As I began molding these young minds into greatness, I started to reflect on my own life and how it could be better. The children confided in me and trusted me, and I needed to stay strong for them. Likewise, my mom had to stay strong for me, because she knew if she lost faith, we both would be on a sinking ship. The children's energy deeply touched me and sometimes left me speechless.

*   *   *

The Butterfly That Couldn't Fly
Because She Couldn't Find Her Way

*You will never know what you meant to me. You struck
my heart like lightning with just one touch and left my
body vitalized and thirsting for more of your strength. Each
step that I took, I wanted to belong to a "whole."*

*You came with open arms, a warm heart, and a helping hand. You
provided me with the things that I desire the most in my time of need.
Your open arms embraced me and gave me support because you knew I
couldn't stand on my own. Your heart was promising and taught me how
to love again and forgive. Your helping hands pointed me to a new oasis.*

*All it took was some time for my mind, body, and soul to revive. You
brighten my day with your strength, beautiful and colorful as the rainbow.*

*You illuminate my life. Once your role was over, you vanished
in thin air. Your footprints will forever be embedded in
my heart. Your faith will never be forgotten. You gave
me wings that I didn't know I had to fly away.*

You were my faith when I didn't have any.

*   *   *

Along the way, I met a vibrant woman filled with determination and energy. Monique exudes confidence in everything she does. She set the framework for things I achieved later down the road in my career. She stands up for what she believes in, even though she knows that she maybe is on the losing side of the battlefield. She plays the role of a devil's advocate. She leads a school, runs a business, and juggles time to spend with family and loved ones. These were the very dreams I had for my life but somehow could not obtain.

The choices we make will always influence our decisions. Along with my mother, Monique played a vital role in the transition from where I was to where I wanted to be. I was fortunate to have these two strong women who fought for life and always created win-win situations. They come from different real-life experiences and cultural backgrounds, but they have the same goals in life. They envisioned success and used their drive and passion to earn it. They both made an effort to help me succeed by giving me the support, love, and, encouragement that I needed to be successful.

Monique knew nothing about me but saw that my intentions were good. At the time, I could not see what she saw in me. By tapping into her life, I began to see things on a whole other level. She encouraged me to reach higher because she believed in my potential. She frankly expressed to me that I had not placed value on my own worth. Once upon a time, I held myself in high esteem and I was certain of my self-worth. Trials and tribulations made me lose that along the way. She challenged me to explore other options. I used her criticisms to teach me the strength that I needed to fight my battles.

Monique recommended a change in my character so that I would not be taken advantage of. She provided a model for me to follow so I could locate information for myself. She was the epitome of tomorrow bringing better things. I learned through Monique not to let the past dictate my future. The key lesson was to create new memories and not fixate on old ones.

I became the captain of my ship. Working with the youths sparked my imagination and reignited my life's aspirations. I immediately gravitated toward these children because they each had a story to tell at such a young age. I realized what I had gone through was nothing compared to some of what they had encountered and had to cope with on a day-to-day basis. Providing support and showing the children that I cared became my priority.

It was important that the children had an outlet to get their emotions across. I gave them what I desperately wished I could have had during my ordeal. It was my responsibility to take these children safely on their journey. Together, we got through our issues. I realized that life was worth living because the children were counting on me. Education was where I belonged.

*   *   *

Hope

I walked into the room
Failure written on my face
Blank stares
In need of direction - A role model
/ Someone to direct and lead me
A place I could call home
A listening ear
I needed support, strength
but most importantly
Love
My vision was clouded with thoughts of the past.
After any storm, there comes a calm.

*   *   *

Finding someone new was the least of my worries. I was not ready to start anything new unless I was emotionally stable. I was very cautious when making decisions, since I had learned from experience that poor judgment may result in falling into the same trap again. I seldom have the urge to venture into the dating world, since I was brought up in a home where dating was not allowed. I still fear being persecuted by my parents and society.

As a young woman brought up in a strict Hindu home, I was taught abstinence and respect for family, morals, and culture. My mind would be filled with guilt if I dared to venture into anything that is "not permitted" or is considered "not right." I have always been a good child in my parent's eyes. My only duties were to attend school and follow my goals.

I invested valuable time into my marriage that can never be regained.

In life, one needs to be egotistical and make a mad dash toward one's life's desires. Do not allow pity and empathy for another person's feelings take custody of happiness. Treat yourself like a priceless gem just in case no one else will. I sought after happiness from my ex-husband by putting his happiness before mine. Now all I have left are memories of the progress I made in his life rather than my own. But later on in life, I know that I will reap the fruits I sowed. Relationships are karmic.

It was unfortunate that I experienced the situation I went through. Hopefully, families who put their children into arranged marriages take into consideration what works for each child's personal needs. Caution must be taken when becoming seriously committed to another person. Looking back, I think knowing some more about Kevin would have helped me to figure out whether he was right for me.

Once an individual enters an arranged marriage, it is his or her responsibility to make it work no matter what, which is not fair on either party. Before long, I realized that arranged marriage nowadays is not as it used to be when my parents were growing up. Things have changed. Couples are not as committed to mending a broken relationship. They tend to instantly switch partners once things are not going the way they would like.

What resonate in my mind are the women in Guyana who attempt to end their own lives because of their husbands' adulterous acts. These women feel that by prematurely ending their lives, they will gain the freedom and escape they long for. Others stay in their marriages because they feel there is no other choice and really believe they cannot leave.

I never understood this until now, years later. Because I am older and have gained wisdom, I understand and can relate to what these women were encountering and how they felt. They probably weren't as fortunate as I am to have a strong individual to stand by their sides in their darkest moments. People coming to America for a better life have to learn that the culture here is extremely different. Although immigrants strive to maintain their own cultural values and traditions, things may not always work out that way.

Chapter 6

A Mother's Worst Nightmare: In Sharmela's Own Words

I have walked down those long, dreary, never-ending roads once before feeling helpless and hopeless. Not being able to voice my opinion and live independently. Young and bethrothed into marriage at the age of 16. A housewife and mother of three before I was 21. My childhood was practically stolen from me when I was blessed with raising a family of my own.

Nowadays, children in America are midway through high school by age 16 and graduating out of college by age 21. Education was not an option for me when I was growing up. Marriage and raising a family was the only choice available to me in my era. These directives were given to me by my parents. After taking my vows at the alter, my life has been a roller coaster ride. I prayed to God that my experiences would never be repeated and that I would live to see my children, especially my daughters, in their adult years entering into happy and healthy marriages.

Luckily, my marriage was one that grew into love and understanding over the years. The problem lies within the cultural realm and dynamics, where women are viewed as second-class citizens. There seems to be a power struggle between men and women. Husbands are normally given the role of bread winners and sole providers. Being a housewife was a full-time job within my marriage. I had to wake up early to cook for my husband and see him off to work, then make meals for the kids and see them off to school. Since my husband's salary was too little to support a family of five, I planted a vegetable garden and my husband took a second job as a fisherman. Our efforts afforded us the supplemental income that we desperately needed to raise our family.

My husband and I worked collectively to weather the storms so we could provide for our family. As a victim of abandonment, Shivani's situation hit home. It felt as though I was reliving my past but this time my daughter was not only abandoned but abused as well. I did everything in my power to provide a safe home and secure a future for my children. I made it a priority to send Shivani to college so that, even if she was by herself or in a relationship, she could make it on her own and provide for herself independently.

This was something I never had. I relied on the earnest paycheck of my husband, which was merely enough for a family our size. There was nothing extra for me to splurge with. I made it my priority to prevent her from thinking about boyfriends or socializing with anything that would distract her from her studies and adulterate her mind. I wanted to be in charge of her love life because I wanted to ensure that she did not step out of bound. I did not want her to stray away from tradition. So, I made Mandir a priority in my home.

Although I was fully aware of the complexities that existed in our society and aware of the paradigm shift took place within families, I was destined to find the perfect husband for Shivani. My intentions were to ensure their abilities to make life changing decisions based on the principles and fundamental belief of Hindus. Much to my dismay, this is not what Shivani encountered during her marriage with Kevin. It had not dawned on me that perhaps their common beliefs were not as mutual as I thought it was.

Darkness had solemnly taken over my sanity and I could not come to grip with how this man was treating my daughter. Being a woman of tradition and a strong believer in Santan Vedic Dharma, I truly believed that all men who followed these scriptures spoke the truth and was free of evil thoughts and vengeance. All true followers know the consequences that comes along with committing such a sin. Then, I was so blinded and did not see the writing on the walls. I could not believe that I have coerced my daughter into this web of adversity. I feel that I have cheated Shivani out of a possibly happy life. Perhaps if I trusted Shivani to make her own decisions, then she would have ended up with the man of her dreams instead of being with a man driven by hatred.

At the time, I was very confident that I had made the right choice by choosing Kevin. He appeared simple, displayed poise, and followed customary gestures and traditional beliefs. Kevin definitely earned my blessings at the altar. But it did not take me long to realize that choosing Kevin to be my daughter's life long partner was not the smartest decision. He came with extra baggage and I had now given my daughter this baggage of family issues, unemployment, health and manic issues. I had fulfilled my duties, which were to see my daughter married off to a man whom I thought could make an honest living because he stated he was a hard worker and devoted to our faith. I find myself asking, "was the arrangement all worth it?" Now I realized that I was asking too much of a 22 year old, who barely experienced life.

*   *   *

The abuse was evident, from her swollen body parts, cuts and scrapes, and a black eye. This was enough to have my body fuming and burst out with anger. I became confrontational while questioning Kevin about my daughter's body scars and drastic weight loss. My quest for answers left me only with assumptions. It seemed as though she was covering up for Kevin and the relationship I had with my daughter began to drift apart.

Shivani's transformation was evident. She was isolated from families, friends and practically vanished. Her personality changed too. One of my mistakes was not taking my daughter's desires into account. I was selfish and inconsiderate. The fear of losing the family she loved was devastating to her so she stayed in her marriage in order not to dishonor her family values.

Shivani knew how deeply I desired her marriage to work so she held on to her marriage tightly. After I found out that my daughter was pregnant, the thought of being grandparents excited my husband and I. But this excitement was overshadowed by the abuse that was taking place in Shivani's household. She didn't want to disappoint us and thought the baby would change his behavior. However, this ordeal became daunting and one I could bear witness to.

I will never forget Shivani's phone calls to me, crying her heart out and asking if I can go to the clinic with her. Of course, she knew I would not endorse such acts that Kevin was determined for her to commit. I even met with the couple and offered to help with raising the child. Kevin immediately expressed that he didn't want the child. I was mortified and wondered the reason behind his logic. Could it have been that the baby would have given him responsibilities and make him think like a man? Or did he have intentions on leaving Shivani after his naturalization so he didn't want any extra baggage to care for or to pay child support? Shivani was in a vulnerable state where she needed a friend she can trust. Her actions said it all. She became very nervous and indecisive. I was then faced with the decision to care for my daughter and put my own personal desires for her to the side. I endorsed her decision and helped her through her journey. I was no longer in charge of her decisions because I married her off and put someone else in charge to sail her on her life journey. Instead of sailing her in the right direction, he tirelessly tried to manipulate her.

I was held accountable for arranging her marriage and for not taking heed to the signs that came my way. Did Shivani's experience change my views on arranged marriage? Shivani's situation has definitely taught me a valuable lesson, which is to spend more time listening to my daughter and her wants and needs and pay less attention to my own. I cannot cheat her out of her by dictating her destiny. I should have been the guide that leads her to finding a suitable match. Previously, I had arranged the marriage of my oldest daughter. They have been married for 15 years. She was 21 at the time of marriage. Watching her go through her marriage, there were lots of happiness and joy. Her and her husband share the same values and had similar goals. I was hoping for the same for Shivani.

*   *   *

At that moment, I realized that I must stay strong for her. Not letting her know my inner gut feelings. Over the years, I have always been a staunch believer in my Dharm. So, I quickly turned to the celestial for guidance. It did not take me long after I began on this mission when I found peace of mind and the soul and serenity in the atmosphere. In so doing, Shivani began to feel some relief and comfort from the burden that was placed on her shoulders. I know that God's blessings come in disguise and only he knows what the future holds for us. I was confident that the morals I instilled in Shivani and my divinity to God would help Shivani to emerge out of the predicament she was in.

I clasped my hands at the feet of the immortal, praying for enlightenment and strength by reciting a universal prayer from the Vedas.

Prayer to God
Universal Hindu Prayer

Tumhi Ho Maataa, Pitaa Tumhi Ho

Tumhi Ho Bandhu, Sakha Tumhi Ho

Tumhi Ho Saathi, Tumhi Sahare

Koi Na Apna, Sivaa Tumhare

Dear God, you are my mother and my father.
You are my relative and you are my friend.
You are my companion, you are my support system.
You are the captain and oarsman of my boat.
I am the flower that was unable to bloom, I am the dust of your feet.

Epilogue

This book was written to enlighten parents about the possible outcome of placing their child in an arranged marriage. Although such parents strongly feel they are maintaining tradition, their child's safety may be compromised. Shivani had limited voice in her relationship once things started to get serious between the couple. She gave her power away to her husband from the time she was engaged. Shivani began the battle with faith—she was convinced there would be a light at the end of the tunnel.

Shivani used several coping mechanisms that were culturally appropriate to resolve her abusive relationship. The initial matchmaker, Dan, could not be reached because those bridges were already burned. The culturally-approved mechanisms did not work in Shivani's favor.

There was a power struggle in Shivani's relationship. Shivani was the educated one and provided for her husband. His reaction was a typical one: he belittled her so he could maintain his "manhood" and masculinity. Because of this, she began to lose her confidence and feel unworthy. He won the battle because he was on top. Although Shivani is highly educated, he was successful in manipulating her to think she had no worth.

Shivani felt obligated to stay in the relationship because she was afraid of societal criticisms. When her family saw her pain, their views changed and they advised her to leave. At that point, she was in desperate need of some direction. She had no control of her destiny.

In essence, Shivani's "matchmakers" left her on her own to make the relationship work. Everyone was aware that she was being mistreated.

Likewise, they were aware of Kevin's infidelities. In Shivani's culture, there are no second chances. There is one way—and that is culture and tradition.

Shivani was fortunate and blessed to have discovered her inner strengths and to have risen above it all and left the past behind her. Sharmela is Shivani's "hero" and will forever hold a special place in her heart. She exudes strength and the true bond that exists between a mother and a daughter. Her wishes were to see Shivani blossom into a woman of confidence and follow culture and tradition. Shivani desire was to find happiness and have independence.

Both Shivani and Sharmela depended on each other's strength as they continued their journey to healing.